Learn Microsoft Azure

Build, manage, and scale cloud applications using the Azure ecosystem

Mohamed Wali

BIRMINGHAM - MUMBAI

Learn Microsoft Azure

Commissioning Editor: Pavan Ramchandani
Acquisition Editor: Akshay Jethani
Content Development Editor: Nithin George Varghese
Technical Editor: Komal Karne
Copy Editor: Safis Editing
Project Coordinator: Drashti Panchal
Proofreader: Safis Editing
Indexer: Pratik Shirodkar
Graphics: Tom Scaria
Production Coordinator: Pratik Shirodkar

First published: December 2018

Production reference: 1241218

Published by Packt Publishing Ltd.
Livery Place
35 Livery Street
Birmingham
B3 2PB, UK.

ISBN 978-1-78961-758-0

www.packtpub.com

mapt.io

Mapt is an online digital library that gives you full access to over 5,000 books and videos, as well as industry leading tools to help you plan your personal development and advance your career. For more information, please visit our website.

Why subscribe?

- Spend less time learning and more time coding with practical eBooks and Videos from over 4,000 industry professionals

- Improve your learning with Skill Plans built especially for you

- Get a free eBook or video every month

- Mapt is fully searchable

- Copy and paste, print, and bookmark content

Packt.com

Did you know that Packt offers eBook versions of every book published, with PDF and ePub files available? You can upgrade to the eBook version at www.packt.com and as a print book customer, you are entitled to a discount on the eBook copy. Get in touch with us at customercare@packtpub.com for more details.

At www.packt.com, you can also read a collection of free technical articles, sign up for a range of free newsletters, and receive exclusive discounts and offers on Packt books and eBooks.

Contributors

About the author

Mohamed Wali is a cloud DevOps engineer based in Amsterdam who has been working with Microsoft technologies for around seven years. He has been working with Azure since 2013. In July 2014, Mohamed became recognized as the youngest Microsoft MVP in the world. He has already authored and co-authored multiple books about Microsoft Azure. He shares his knowledge and expertise through blogging, authoring books, and speaking at events.

This book would not have seen the light without the help of many people—Akshay Jethani, Komal Karne, Nithin George, and the other contributors at Packt Publishing.

A special thanks to Sjoukje Zaal for her valuable reviews since my first book. Mohamed Fawzi, cloud architect at Microsoft, and Mahmoud Dwidar, CTO of BlueCloud Technologies, have always encouraged and pushed me forward throughout my career, leading to this moment.

About the reviewer

Sjoukje Zaal is a Principal Expert Microsoft and Microsoft Azure MVP with over 15 years of experience of providing architecture, development, consultancy and design expertise. She works at Ordina, a system integrator based in the Netherlands.

She is active in the Microsoft community as a co-founder of SP&C NL and MixUG, a writer, a public speaker, and is also active on MSDN.

Packt is searching for authors like you

If you're interested in becoming an author for Packt, please visit `authors.packtpub.com` and apply today. We have worked with thousands of developers and tech professionals, just like you, to help them share their insight with the global tech community. You can make a general application, apply for a specific hot topic that we are recruiting an author for, or submit your own idea.

Table of Contents

Preface   1

Chapter 1: Microsoft Azure 101   5
  Microsoft Azure overview   6
    Evolution of cloud computing   6
    Azure as a cloud platform   8
    Cloud deployment models   8
      Private cloud   8
        Advantages   9
        Disadvantages   9
      Public cloud   9
        Advantages   9
        Disadvantages   10
      Hybrid cloud   10
    Azure regions   10
      Public regions   10
      Azure Government   12
      Azure Germany   12
      Azure China   12
    Azure subscriptions   13
  Cloud services   14
  Azure portal experience   15
    Signing up for a free Azure subscription   15
    The portal   16
      The dashboard   17
      The hub   19
      Notifications   21
      Azure cloud shell   22
      Azure portal settings   23
      More to do in the portal   26
  Azure Resource Manager model   27
    ARM key points   28
  Azure automation tools   28
    Azure PowerShell   29
      Installing the Azure PowerShell module   29
      Installing the Azure PowerShell module from the PowerShell Gallery   29
    Azure CLI   30
      Installing Azure CLI 2.0   30
  Summary   32
  Questions   33
  Further reading   33

Chapter 2: Understanding Azure Storage   35
  Introduction to Microsoft Azure Storage   35
    Why use Azure Storage?   36
  Azure Storage types   36
    Durability   36
      Replication types   37
        Locally redundant storage   37
        Zone redundant storage   38
        Geo-redundant storage   39
        Read-access geo-redundant storage   39
    Performance   40
      Standard storage   40
      Premium storage   40
    Persistency   40
      Persistent storage   40
      Non-persistent storage   40
  Azure storage accounts   41
    General-purpose storage account v1   41
    Blob storage account   41
      Hot access tier   42
      Cool access tier   42
      Archive access tier   42
      Premium access tier   42
    General-purpose storage account v2   42
    Azure Storage account tips   42
  Creating an Azure storage account   43
  Azure Storage services   47
    Blob storage   47
      Creating Blob storage   48
      Blob storage key points   53
    Table storage   54
      PartitionKey   55
      RowKey   55
      Timestamp   55
      Creating Table storage   56
      Table storage key points   58
    Queue storage   59
      Creating Queue storage   60
      Queue storage key points   62
    File storage   63
      File storage advantages   63
      Creating file storage   64
      File storage key points   68
  Azure Storage architecture   68
    Frontend layer   69
    Partition layer   69
    Stream layer   69
    Sparse storage and TRIM in Azure   69

Summary 70
Questions 70
Further reading 71
Chapter 3: Getting Familiar with Azure Virtual Networks 73
  An introduction to Azure Virtual Networks 73
    What is Azure VNet? 74
    Why use Azure VNets? 74
    Creating an Azure VNet 75
    Adding subnets to the VNet 78
      Adding a normal subnet to the VNet 78
      Adding a gateway subnet to the VNet 81
    Adding an address space to the Azure VNet 82
  Azure VNet related services 83
    Public IPs 83
      Creating a public IP address 84
      Creating a public IP prefix 87
    NICs 89
    Azure service endpoints 92
  Summary 92
  Questions 93
  Further reading 93
Chapter 4: Understanding Azure Virtual Machines 95
  Introducing Azure virtual machines 96
    Azure VM statuses 96
    Azure VM service level agreements 97
    Azure VM series 98
  Creating an Azure VM 99
  Azure VM storage 111
    Managed versus unmanaged disks 111
      Managed Disks-key points 111
    VM disks 113
      Adding a data disk to an Azure VM 115
        Data disk-key points 120
      Expanding disks 120
      Host caching 121
        Host caching-key points 122
  Azure VM networking 122
    Adding inbound and outbound rules 123
    Adding an additional network interface card to the VM 124
    Configuring the NICs 126
    Azure VNet considerations for Azure VMs 130
  Summary 131
  Questions 131
  Further reading 132

Chapter 5: Azure Web Apps Basics   133
Introduction to Azure App Service   133
Azure Web Apps   134
App Service plans   134
Azure App Service Environments   135
App Service Environment types   136
Creating an App Service Environment   137
Creating an App Service plan   141
Creating an App Service   145
Summary   150
Questions   151
Further reading   151

Chapter 6: Managing Azure Web Apps   153
Deployment slots   153
Deployment slots key points   155
App Service application settings   156
Application settings key points   160
Azure App Service scalability   161
Scaling up   161
App Service plan scaleup key points   163
Scaling out   164
Scaling out the App Service plan manually   164
Scaling out the App Service plan automatically   165
Key points for autoscaling your App Service plan   170
Azure App Service backup   171
App Service backup key points   173
Summary   173
Questions   173
Further reading   174

Chapter 7: Basics of Azure SQL Database   175
Introduction to Azure SQL Database   175
Why Azure SQL Database?   175
SQL Database (IaaS/PaaS)   177
Azure SQL Database (PaaS)   177
Scenarios that would fit Azure SQL Database   177
SQL on Azure VMs (IaaS)   177
Scenarios that would suit SQL on Azure VMs   178
Azure SQL Database types   178
Elastic database pools   178
Single databases   178
SQL database managed instance   179
Service tier types   179
DTU service tiers   179

vCore service tiers   180
Creating an Azure SQL Database   181
Connecting to Azure SQL Database   187
Server-level firewall   188
Connecting to Azure SQL Database using SQL SSMS   190
Summary   192
Questions   192
Further reading   193

Chapter 8: Managing Azure SQL Database   195
Azure SQL elastic database pools   195
Benefits of using elastic database pools   195
Creating an elastic database pool   196
Adding a database to an elastic pool   198
Setting Azure Active Directory authentication   201
Azure SQL Database business continuity   205
How business continuity works in Azure SQL Database   205
Hardware failure   206
Point-in-time restore   206
Point-in-time restoration key points   209
Restoring a deleted database   209
Active geo-replication   211
Auto-failover groups   214
Azure SQL Managed Instances   216
Azure SQL Managed Instance types   216
Creating an Azure SQL Managed Instance   217
Connecting to an Azure SQL Managed Instance   219
Azure SQL Managed Instance key points   219
Summary   220
Questions   220
Further reading   221

Chapter 9: Understanding Azure Active Directory   223
Introduction to Azure AD   223
Azure AD benefits   224
Azure AD flavors   225
Free   225
Basic   225
Premium P1   225
Premium P2   226
Working with users in Azure AD   226
Creating an Azure AD user   226
User password reset   232
Deleted users   233
Working with groups in Azure AD   234
Creating an Azure AD group   234

Azure AD common tasks 240
  Self-service password reset 240
  Azure AD user sign-in activities 244
  Multi-Factor Authentication 246
  Configuring a custom domain name in Azure AD 248
Summary 250
Questions 251
Further reading 251

Chapter 10: Monitoring and Automating Azure Services Using OMS 253
  Introduction to OMS 253
    OMS terminologies 254
  Introduction to Azure Log Analytics 255
    Azure Log Analytics deployment models 255
  Onboarding OMS agents 255
    Creating the workspace 256
    Onboarding the agents 258
    Adding solutions to the workspace 269
  Azure Automation 275
    Benefits of Azure Automation 275
    Azure Automation runbook types 275
    Creating an automation account 276
    Azure runbooks 279
    Azure Automation hybrid integration 283
  Summary 285
  Questions 286
  Further reading 286

Chapter 11: Data Protection and Business Continuity Using OMS 287
  Introducing Azure Recovery Services 287
    Introducing to Azure Backup 288
      Why Azure Backup? 289
    Introducing to Azure Site Recovery 290
      ASR supportability 290
        Hyper-V servers 290
        VMware vSphere and physical servers 293
  Implementing Azure Backup 295
    Creating an Azure Recovery Services vault 295
    Backing up an Azure VM 298
  Implementing Azure Site Recovery 304
    Preparing the infrastructure for replication 304
    Enabling the replication 319
  Summary 323
  Questions 324
  Further reading 324

Assessments   325

Other Books You May Enjoy   329

Index   333

Preface

Cloud computing has been a buzzphrase for a while. Now, companies are moving to the cloud in droves, and learning one of the most commonly used cloud platforms is becoming a necessity for anyone working in IT.

Within this book, you will learn about the most common used services in Azure, such as Azure Storage, Azure Networks, Azure VMs, Azure Web Apps, Azure SQL Databases, Azure Active Directory, and OMS.

Who this book is for

Learn Microsoft Azure is for system administrators, cloud engineers, and developers who want to get started with using Azure as their cloud platform and build cloud-based applications for their enterprises.

What this book covers

Chapter 1, *Microsoft Azure 101*, introduces you to Azure, giving you a quick introduction to cloud computing, its types, and the Azure portal.

Chapter 2, *Understanding Azure Storage*, covers Azure Storage, looking at its importance, architecture, its types and the differences between them, and how and when to use it.

Chapter 3, *Getting Familiar with Azure Virtual Networks*, goes through Azure Virtual Networks, its components, and how to work with theme.

Chapter 4, *Understanding Azure Virtual Machines*, explains how to work with Azure VMs and establish a complete IaaS solution.

Chapter 5, *Starting with Azure Web Apps Basics*, covers one of Azure App Service, its different types, and how to work with them.

Chapter 6, *Managing Azure Web Apps*, covers some of the highly available solutions for Azure Web Apps in this chapter.

Chapter 7, *Basics of Azure SQL Database*, explores the Azure SQL Database, its types, and how to deploy it in Azure.

Chapter 8, *Managing Azure SQL Database*, covers other Azure SQL Database types and explains how to provide a highly available solution for them.

Chapter 9, *Understanding Azure Active Directory*, introduces Azure AD and explains how to work with it as an identity solution to manage your environment.

Chapter 10, *Monitoring and Automating Azure Services Using OMS*, introduces OMS and walks through two of its types: Azure Log Analytics and Azure Automation.

Chapter 11, *Data Protection and Business Continuity Using OMS*, explains how to provide data protection and business continuity to your infrastructure using Azure Backup and Azure Site Recovery, which are part of OMS.

To get the most out of this book

A basic knowledge of virtualization, networks, web development, databases, and active directory is required to get the most out of this book.

Download the color images

We also provide a PDF file that has color images of the screenshots/diagrams used in this book. You can download it here: https://www.packtpub.com/sites/default/files/downloads/9781789617580_ColorImages.pdf.

Conventions used

There are a number of text conventions used throughout this book.

CodeInText: Indicates code words in text, database table names, folder names, filenames, file extensions, pathnames, dummy URLs, user input, and Twitter handles. Here is an example: "In the search bar, write storage account."

Warnings or important notes appear like this.

Tips and tricks appear like this.

Get in touch

Feedback from our readers is always welcome.

General feedback: If you have questions about any aspect of this book, mention the book title in the subject of your message and email us at customercare@packtpub.com.

Errata: Although we have taken every care to ensure the accuracy of our content, mistakes do happen. If you have found a mistake in this book, we would be grateful if you would report this to us. Please visit www.packt.com/submit-errata, selecting your book, clicking on the Errata Submission Form link, and entering the details.

Piracy: If you come across any illegal copies of our works in any form on the internet, we would be grateful if you would provide us with the location address or website name. Please contact us at copyright@packt.com with a link to the material.

If you are interested in becoming an author: If there is a topic that you have expertise in and you are interested in either writing or contributing to a book, please visit authors.packtpub.com.

Reviews

Please leave a review. Once you have read and used this book, why not leave a review on the site that you purchased it from? Potential readers can then see and use your unbiased opinion to make purchase decisions, we at Packt can understand what you think about our products, and our authors can see your feedback on their book. Thank you!

For more information about Packt, please visit packt.com.

Microsoft Azure 101

Azure is one of the leading public cloud service providers. Microsoft Azure is a cloud computing platform that helps you build, deploy, and manage applications to overcome your business challenges. This journey starts with the fundamentals of cloud computing and moves on to explaining the configuration of Azure infrastructure, exploring Azure services, and working on **virtual memory systems (VMS)** and deployment models in Azure. You will also see how to secure and troubleshoot your Azure cloud environment and many more exciting features, in order to be fully aware of best practices for Azure cloud administration. Let's cut to the chase and see what we have in this introductory chapter, *Microsoft Azure 101*. This chapter will introduce cloud computing to you and describe its evolution, the types of cloud deployment models, and the cloud services that Azure provides. After that, we'll walk through the Azure portal, introducing its components. Then, we'll discuss the Azure Resource Manager model used by Azure. Finally, you will learn about the different tools you can use to automate your tasks with Azure.

Briefly, the following topics will be covered in this chapter:

- Microsoft Azure overview
- Cloud service types
- Azure portal experience
- Azure Resource Manager model
- Azure automation tools

Microsoft Azure overview

In this section, you will be introduced to cloud computing and Microsoft Azure.

Evolution of cloud computing

Modern computing technology has been around since the 1950s. We have witnessed many changes so far.

The journey started when we had physical servers that we used to operate our enterprise applications on, but companies were getting bigger and the requirements of the applications were getting greater. That meant buying more and more physical servers to keep up with technology changes and company expansion. As a result, we started to face the following problems:

- More space was needed for physical servers.
- The cost of power usage for the physical servers and air conditioning.
- You were not fully utilizing your environment, because every server was acting with one or two server roles, which meant some of each server's resources were wasted.
- The IT operations were not as efficient as they should have been. As a result, you had to hire more system engineers to manage the infrastructure.

These major problems have been targeted by another technology called **virtualization**. This technology has totally changed the game and let us enter a new era of computing. It technology allowed us to run different operating servers on the same server simultaneously and with total isolation.

In a nutshell, this technology made our world better and provided the following advantages:

- **Utilizing hardware resources**: Instead of installing a server that is acting with one role only (that is, a domain controller), you can create another server to act with another role (a SQL server) on the same physical server, until you fully utilize your hardware resources.
- **Saving cost**: You no longer have to buy many new physical servers, since you can use the same physical server for many different purposes. As a result, you will pay less for power, and air-conditioning.

- **Saving space**: You will be able to save space in your company for other purposes, such as using a floor that you used in the past for your physical servers to take on board a new team.
- **Hardware failure resiliency**: If you faced a major issue with the hardware of the physical servers, it would take a long time to get the solution up and running again, but with virtualization, you can have your applications on another server. They are stored in files on the physical servers and can be reused on another physical server to continue operating normally. If you used high availability for your virtualization platform, you will see almost no downtime.

The next step was based on virtualization technology and it was the move to the cloud.

You do not have to care about the hardware, system infrastructure, middleware, and so on, only the stuff you want to use.

Cloud computing offers solutions that will fit every role in an organization. Here are some of its features:

- **Hardware**: Hardware installation and maintenance was a big problem, because even after embracing virtualization technology, we still had our own hardware that we needed to take care of. But with cloud computing, this provide a low-latency is the responsibility of the cloud service provider.
- **Global presence**: Microsoft has many data centers across the globe, which means it can provide low-latency services.
- **On-demand service**: You no longer have to wait for the hardware purchase, the infrastructure preparation, and the application installation, which would take a long time. With cloud computing, you can request the service you wish and it should be up and running in a matter of minutes.
- **Scalability**: When you have load on your cloud services, you can scale them in and out according to your usage.
- **Broad network access**: You can connect to your cloud resources from anywhere in the world using any device with an internet connection and any operating system.
- **Pay as you go**: You only pay for the services that you use.
- **Hybrid compatibility**: Using Azure does not mean you need to give up your on-premises solutions. You can have a hybrid solution that spans on-premises and Azure.

Azure as a cloud platform

Microsoft Azure was announced in October 2008 with the code name *Red Dog* and was officially released in February 2010 with the name *Windows Azure*. It offered web roles and SQL databases. In March 2014, Microsoft rebranded its cloud platform from Windows Azure to Microsoft Azure.

The general availability of Azure and Microsoft has added many services to its platform to fit most customers' needs. It has expanded its data centers to the continents across the globe. The services that Azure supports at the moment include, but are not limited to, the following:

- Mobile services
- Web services
- Compute services
- Storage services
- Messaging
- Network services
- Media services
- Machine learning
- Internet of Things

Cloud deployment models

The cloud is available in different types. The following types are the most common.

Private cloud

In this model, the cloud is exclusively used by a single organization, using its own computing resources. It manages and maintains every piece of the cloud in its own data centers.

Advantages

This model has the following advantages:

- **Customizability**: You can do whatever you want with the services offered via this model, as long as it is technically feasible because you own and manage everything yourself.
- **Not shared**: Sharing the same host that serves your applications and VMs might be a concern for many companies. Some of them may consider it as a security threat. Since you are following the private cloud deployment model, it means you are not sharing anything with anyone.

Disadvantages

This model also has some disadvantages:

- **High costs**: Buying your own hardware/software, managing it, and hiring engineers to take care of that comes with a high price
- **Under-utilization**: Running your own private cloud in a highly available environment means that your environment will be fully utilized and you are paying for more than you actually use

Public cloud

In this model, you are using your services from a cloud service provider that handles the underlying infrastructure of the service you are using. These services are provided via the internet.

Advantages

This model has the following advantages:

- **Unburdening you from most of the operational headache**: You no longer have to operate everything by yourself, because most of the operations are handled by the cloud service provider
- **Scalability**: You can scale your services whenever you wish within a short time with no downtime
- **Lower cost**: You are only paying for what you are using

Disadvantages

This model also has some disadvantages:

- **Security**: Some financial and governmental organizations do not like to host their data in the cloud for security reasons
- **Unpredictable cost**: If you do not have a well-designed cloud solution, you might end up paying too much

Hybrid cloud

As the name of this deployment model indicates, it is a combination of the private cloud and public cloud. In this model, you can span your solutions across your data centers and Azure and get the best of both.

It's quite clear that it has the best of both previous models, but note that the complexity of your solutions will be greater.

Azure regions

As mentioned earlier, Azure has a global presence covering every continent with its data centers. At the time of writing, Azure data centers are available in 54 regions worldwide.

The regions are classified as follows:

- **Public regions**: Available for use by everyone around the globe
- **Azure Government**: Available only for the US government
- **Azure Germany**: Trusted regions by Germany, as it follows the data privacy regulations of Germany
- **Azure China**: Trusted regions by China, as it adheres to Chinese policies and data handling regulations

Public regions

The following table shows all the Azure public regions that Microsoft covers:

Region	Location
East US	Virginia
East US 2	Virginia
Central US	Iowa

North Central US	Illinois
South Central US	Texas
West Central US	Wyoming
West US	California
West US 2	Washington
Canada East	Quebec
Canada Central	Toronto
Brazil South	Sao Paulo
North Europe	Ireland
West Europe	Netherlands
France Central	Paris
France South	Marseille
UK West	Cardiff
UK South	London
Southeast Asia	Singapore
East Asia	Hong Kong
Australia East	New South Wales
Australia Southeast	Victoria
Australia Central	Canberra
Australia Central 2	Canberra
Central India	Pune
West India	Mumbai
South India	Chennai
Japan East	Tokyo, Saitama
Japan West	Osaka
Korea Central	Seoul
Korea South	Busan

Microsoft Azure is expanding its data centers year on year. The following table includes new public regions that are expected to be generally available in the next 1-2 years:

Region	Location
Germany North	Germany North
Germany West Central	Germany West Central
Switzerland North	Zurich
Switzerland West	Geneva
Norway East	Norway
Norway West	Norway
South Africa West	Cape Town

South Africa North	Johannesburg
UAE Central	Abu Dhabi
UAE North	Dubai

Azure Government

The following table shows all the Azure Government regions that Microsoft covers:

Region	Location
US Gov Virginia	Virginia
US Gov Iowa	Iowa
US Gov Arizona	Arizona
US Gov Texas	Texas
US DoD East	Virginia
US DoD Central	Iowa

Microsoft Azure is expanding its data centers year after year. The following table includes new government regions that are expected to be generally available in the next 1-2 years:

Region	Location
US Sec East	Undisclosed
US Sec West	Undisclosed

Azure Germany

The following table shows all the Azure Germany regions that Microsoft covers:

Region	Location
Germany Central	Frankfurt
Germany Northeast	Magdeburg

Azure China

The following table shows all the Azure China regions that Microsoft covers:

Region	Location
China East	Shanghai
China East 2	Shanghai
China North	Beijing
China North 2	Beijing

You can find out the nearest region to you with the lowest latency via the following website: http://www.azurespeed.com/.

Azure services are available in 140 countries around the globe and support 17 languages, and 24 currencies.

For a proper depiction of the previously mentioned Azure regions all around the globe, visit the following link: https://azure.microsoft.com/en-in/global-infrastructure/regions/

Azure subscriptions

Microsoft Azure offers different types of subscriptions that you can use to access Azure services and start playing with them:

- **Free account**: This account offers 200 USD credits that you can use for Azure services within the first 30 days after signing up. If you want to upgrade this subscription after it expires, note that you can keep all of your services up and running.

  After the 30 days pass, it does not mean you can no longer use the same subscription. Actually, you can use it for 12 months from the first day you signed up, but only for the services, at the following URL: https://azure.microsoft.com/en-us/free/.

  But the other paid services will be decommissioned after the first 30-days or the consumption of 200 USD credits.

- **MSDN subscriptions**: If you have an MSDN subscription, you will get a specific amount of Azure credits per month, depending on the subscription type. Note that you can add a credit card to avoid stopping your Azure services if you exceeded the credits you have. The following are the different types of MSDN subscriptions and how much credits per month they have to offer:
  - Visual Studio Professional (standard subscription and annual cloud subscription): $50
  - Visual Studio Test Professional: $50
  - MSDN Platforms: $100

- Visual Studio Enterprise (standard subscription and annual cloud subscription): $150
- Visual Studio Enterprise (MPN): $150
- Visual Studio Enterprise (BizSpark): $150

- **Enterprise agreements**: This type of subscription is meant for enterprises, where you can pay an amount of money upfront for using Azure services throughout the year. This type of subscription gives you great discounts. So, it will be the best solution if you are going to use what you have signed up for, as it will save you a lot of money.
- **Pay as you go**: It's quite clear that with this type of subscription, you are only paying for what you are using via your credit card. You are not committed to using it for a specific period, as you can start it whenever you want and stop it whenever you want.

Cloud services

Microsoft offers different types of cloud service in Azure. The most commonly known services are the following:

- **Infrastructure as a service (IaaS)**: This type of cloud service allows you to run VMs on the cloud. The cloud service provider will take care of the underlying infrastructure, such as hardware, network, storage, and virtualization platform. However, you will be responsible for managing and maintaining what's inside your VM.
- **Platform as a service (PaaS)**: This type of cloud service allows you to run your applications on Azure. The cloud service provider will take care of managing and maintaining the underlying infrastructure. Running your web app/container/microservices on Azure would unburden the headache of the hardware, network, storage, virtualization, operating system, and IIS. You only need to develop your application and run it.
- **Software as a service (SaaS)**: This type of cloud service allows you to use software on the cloud. The cloud service provider will handle the underlying infrastructure, such as hardware, storage, network, virtualization, operating system, and even the application itself. For example, Office 365 provides a variety of solutions ready to be used by you, such as email services, VOIP services, and so on, without implementing Exchange or Skype.

Azure portal experience

Azure offers a wide range of services, and learning the fundamentals on how to do basic management on everything can be scary. The Azure portal provides a consistent experience that covers finding an instance of a resource to performing basic management operations. In this section, we will introduce the Azure portal.

Signing up for a free Azure subscription

Before getting started with the Azure portal, let's create a free subscription that you can use throughout this book:

1. Navigate to `https://azure.microsoft.com/`.
2. Click on **Start free**.
3. You will be navigated to another web page, where you will be asked to start for free or to buy now. We will select **Start free** for the sake of testing throughout this book:

4. After that, you will be redirected to log in using your Microsoft account.
5. Then, you will be asked to enter some personal information, such as your name, country, and phone number. Some verification will be done by phone and credit card.
6. Within a few moments, your Azure account will be ready.

The portal

Once your account has been created, you can login to the Azure portal. The portal can be accessed at `https://portal.azure.com`.

The portal is your way to access and manage your resources in Azure, such as VMs, web apps, SQL databases, and so on. This is the easiest way, but it is not the only way. More ways will be discussed later on in this chapter.

When you first log in the portal, it will look like the following screenshot:

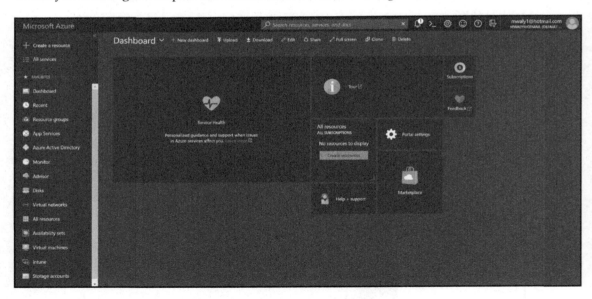

As you can see, this portal consists of many parts. Let's break it down to understand what it consists of.

The dashboard

Every time you open the Azure portal, the first thing you will look at is the dashboard:

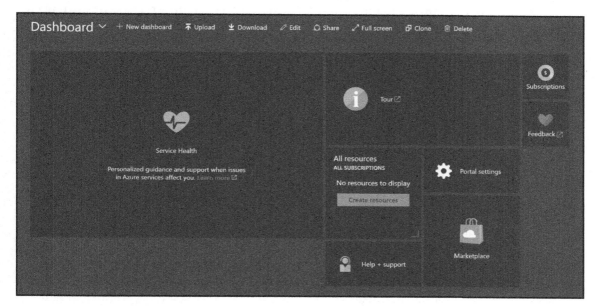

That's why you can pin every Azure service, so you can view what is important to you to in the dashboard. You can easily access it from here, instead of opening it from it is original location.

As you can see in the previous screenshot, you can do the following:

- Create a new dashboard by clicking on the **New dashboard** option.
- You can back up dashboards and reuse them. To back up a dashboard, you need to click on the **Download** option. This will download a JSON file. You can restore the dashboard by clicking on the **Upload** option. This will prompt you to specify the JSON file of the dashboard you want to restore.
- To edit the dashboard to resize the tiles, delete it, or change its location, you have to click on the **Edit** option.
- When you have a dashboard, you might want to share it with someone else. To do so, you need to click on the **Share** option. This will ask you whether you want to publish it or not, and then you can control who will access it.
- You can also have the dashboard in full screen mode by clicking on **Full screen** option.
- If you want to have a copy of the dashboard to manipulate or test something new in the meantime, you will want to keep the dashboard intact for people to access it. You can clone it by clicking on the **Clone** option. This will make a copy of the dashboard.
- If you no longer need a dashboard, you can delete it by clicking on the **Delete** option. This will ask for a confirmation that you want to delete the dashboard.
- In case you have more than one dashboard and want to navigate between them, you can click on the **Dashboard** option. This will open a drop-down list with all the existing dashboards, and then you can click on the one you want to navigate to.

The hub

This is the column you can see in the left-hand menu when you log in to the Azure portal. It displays Azure services in a more organized way. For example, if you created some VMs, you can view and manage them by clicking on **Virtual machines** in the hub, and the same goes for the other services, as shown in the following screenshot:

You will note that not all the services are displayed in the left menu. In order to display all of them, click on **All services**, and you can use the filter to narrow down your search for the service you want:

As you can see in the preceding screenshot, there are stars and circles. The stars are pinned to the main hub; the circles are not. So, you can select what is to be displayed to make your access to the services much easier.

The window that pops up when you click on one of the Azure services in the Azure portal, such as **Virtual machines** is called a blade.

A set of blades or chain of selections is called a **journey**. For instance, when you select **Virtual machines** inside the Azure portal, click on an existing virtual machine and then select its settings.

Notifications

If you are creating, modifying, or deleting an Azure resource, or if there's any update from Microsoft related to Azure services, you will note all of that in the **Notifications** pane. You can open it by clicking on the bell in the top-right side of the portal:

Azure cloud shell

This is an interactive shell that can enable you to manage Azure services either via PowerShell for Windows users or Bash for Linux users.

At the time of writing, using PowerShell in the Azure Cloud Shell was in preview. You can access it from the portal, as shown in the following screenshot:

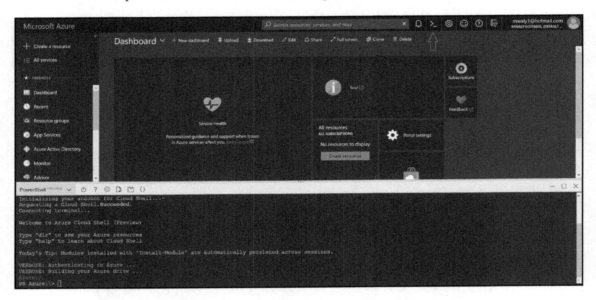

Azure portal settings

You can manage the settings of the portal by clicking on the gear icon on the top-right of the portal, as shown in the following screenshot:

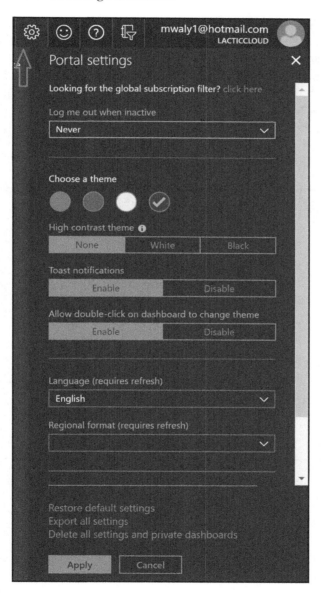

As shown in the previous screenshot, you can control the following:

- **Log me out when inactive**: You can define how long it will take to sign out from the portal when you are not active in it any more. For security reasons, you need to consider this.
- **Choose a theme**: You can change the theme of the portal according to the colors displayed in the previous screenshot. You can select a color that will make you comfortable while working in the Azure portal.
- **High contrast theme**: Using a high contrast theme overrides the theme selection you made in the previous step. You are only allowed to navigate among the following options:
  - **None**: This will not impact the theme selection.
  - **White**: This will make the portal very white, as shown in the following screenshot:

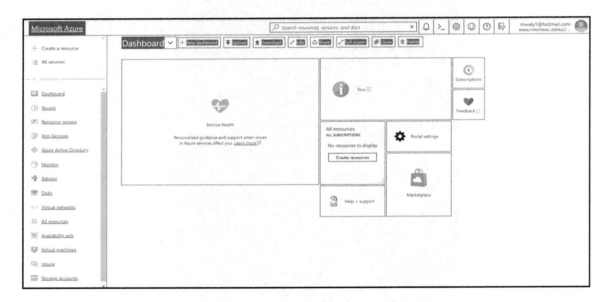

- **Black:** This will make the portal very black, as shown in the following screenshot:

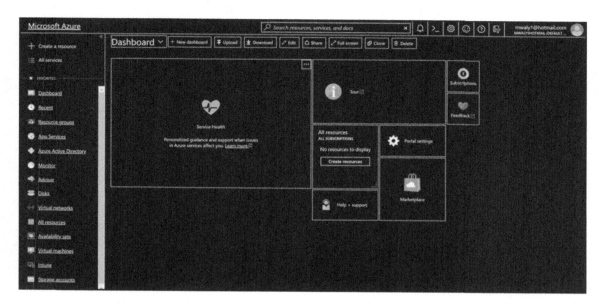

- **Toast notifications**: In the notifications section, I've illustrated that when you create, modify, or delete any Azure resource, you will receive notifications. These notifications can be displayed by clicking on the bell, but at the time the process happens you will receive a toast notification, as shown in the following screenshot:

 If you disable toast notifications, you will be able to see the notifications under the bell icon, but nothing will pop up during the process to notify you.

- **Allow a double-click on dashboard to change the theme**: As this setting indicates, you can change the theme of the portal by double-clicking, which is enabled by default. You can disable it if you wish.
- **Language**: Specify the language of the portal.
- **Regional format (requires refresh)**: You can select a regional format for the language according to the country you are living in. For example, if you are living in Australia, then the language will be English. In this setting, you can select a regional format (English Australia).

More to do in the portal

There are more things to do in the portal, such as the following:

- You can send feedback by clicking on the ☺ symbol in the top-right.
- You can request help and support by clicking on the ? symbol.
- If you have more than one directory or subscription, you can filter them by clicking on the symbol.
- By clicking on the account that you are using in the top-right of the portal, you can sign out, change the password, view your contact information, and more, as shown in the following screenshot:

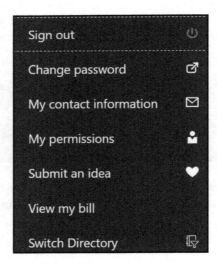

Azure Resource Manager model

In 2014, Microsoft launched a new portal that follows a new model, called the **Azure Resource Manager (ARM)** model.

This model depends on the concept of resource groups, which means you can group all your resources within a container, resulting in resources being deployed in parallel.

The following diagram describes the resources deployed through the ARM model:

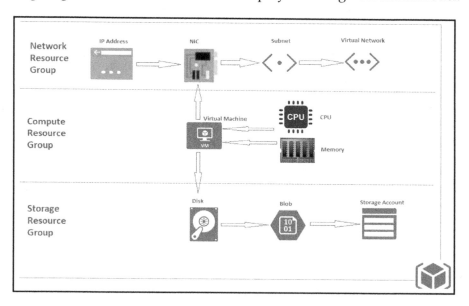

Here are the benefits you will gain by using the ARM model:

- Ability to manage your resources as a group instead of managing them separately.
- Using **role-based access control (RBAC)** to control access to resources, so that you can assign permissions to a user on a resource or some resources, but not to other resources (as it was in the classic portal).
- Using tags to organize and classify your resources, which can help you with billing. For example, you might want to monitor the billing of some resources that make up a solution, such as a web server. By assigning a tag to the resources that make up that solution, you will be able to monitor the billing.

- Support the use of JSON to deploy resources instead of using the portal:
    - Deploy resources in parallel instead of deploying them sequentially, and wait until each resource deployment finishes to deploy another one.
    - Specify dependencies during resources deployment. For example, a VM will not be created until a storage account and a virtual network gets deployed, because the VM VHD will need a place to be stored in an IP address from a virtual network.
    - Reuse the JSON template to deploy solutions with the same specifications.

ARM key points

For a better understanding of the ARM model, you should consider the following key points:

- Resources with the same life cycle should be gathered in the same resource group
- Resources in different regions can be in the same resource group
- Every resource must be assigned to a resource group, so whenever you want to move a resource between resource groups, you must remove it from its current resource group and then add it to the new resource group
- Resource groups support RBAC, where a user can get access to specific resources, and have no access to the others
- Some resources can be shared across resource groups, such as storage accounts
- Every resource must be assigned to a resource group, so whenever you want to move a resource between resource groups, you must remove it from its current resource group, and then add it to the new resource group

Azure automation tools

It is no surprise that we commonly face repetitive and time-consuming tasks. For example, you might want to create multiple virtual machines. You would have to follow the previous guide multiple times to get your job done. This is why Microsoft supports its Azure services with multiple ways of automating most of the tasks that can be implemented in Azure.

Azure PowerShell

PowerShell is commonly used with most Microsoft products, and Azure is no less important than any of these products. You can use Azure PowerShell cmdlets to manage most Azure services.

Installing the Azure PowerShell module

There are two ways of installing the Azure PowerShell module on Windows:

- Download and install the module from the following link: https://www.microsoft.com/web/downloads/platform.aspx
- Install the module from the PowerShell Gallery

Installing the Azure PowerShell module from the PowerShell Gallery

The following are the steps required to get Azure PowerShell installed:

1. Open PowerShell in an elevated mode.
2. To install the Azure PowerShell module for the current portal, run the following cmdlet:

   ```
   Install-Module AzureRM
   ```

   If your PowerShell requires a NuGet provider, you will be asked to agree to install it, and you will have to agree to the installation policy modification, as the repository is not available in your environment, as shown in the following screenshot:

```
Administrator: Windows PowerShell                                               —   □   ×
Windows PowerShell
Copyright (C) 2016 Microsoft Corporation. All rights reserved.

PS C:\WINDOWS\system32> Install-Module AzureRM

NuGet provider is required to continue
PowerShellGet requires NuGet provider version '2.8.5.201' or newer to interact with NuGet-based repositories. The NuGet
provider must be available in 'C:\Program Files\PackageManagement\ProviderAssemblies' or 'C:\Users\Mohamed
Waly\AppData\Local\PackageManagement\ProviderAssemblies'. You can also install the NuGet provider by running
'Install-PackageProvider -Name NuGet -MinimumVersion 2.8.5.201 -Force'. Do you want PowerShellGet to install and import the
NuGet provider now?
[Y] Yes  [N] No  [S] Suspend  [?] Help (default is "Y"): y

Untrusted repository
You are installing the modules from an untrusted repository. If you trust this repository, change its InstallationPolicy
value by running the Set-PSRepository cmdlet. Are you sure you want to install the modules from 'PSGallery'?
[Y] Yes  [A] Yes to All  [N] No  [L] No to All  [S] Suspend  [?] Help (default is "N"): y
```

Azure CLI

The Azure CLI is an open source and cross-platform tool that supports implementing all the tasks you can do in the Azure portal with commands. This tool can be used to provide automation by writing all the tasks you want to configure in the Azure CLI and running it instead of manually doing it over and over again. It can be used to run on Windows, Linux, and macOS. The latest version is Azure CLI 2.0.

Installing Azure CLI 2.0

Perform the following steps to install Azure CLI 2.0:

1. Download Azure CLI 2.0 from the following link: `https://azurecliprod.azureedge.net/msi/azure-cli-2.0.47.msi`.

2. Once downloaded, you can start the installation:

3. Once you click on **Install**, it will start to validate your environment to check whether it is compatible with it or not. Then, it starts the installation:

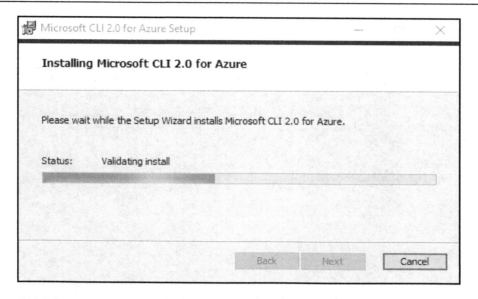

4. Once the installation completes, you can click on **Finish**, and you are good to go:

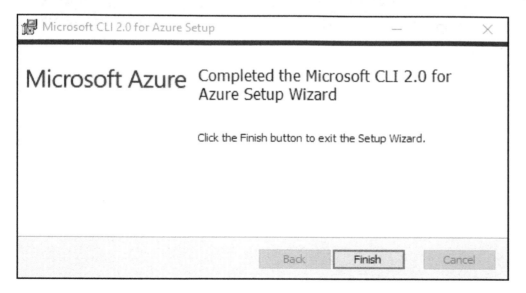

5. Once done, you can open Command Prompt and write `az` to access Azure the CLI commands:

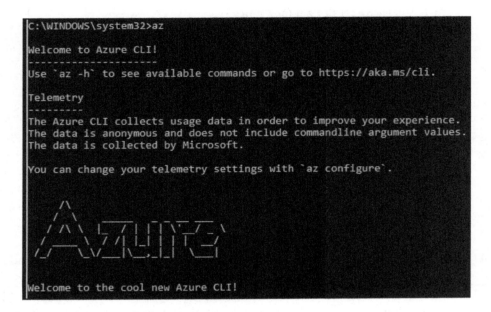

Summary

So far, we have covered some preliminary subject matter regarding cloud computing generally, and Azure specifically. This chapter can be considered as the foundation for the coming chapters.

In the next chapter, covering Azure Storage, its importance, types, and so on will be dealt with. Therefore, the knowledge gained in this chapter is required for a better understanding of the coming chapters.

Questions

1. Virtualization is considered as the foundation of the cloud. (True | False)
2. The cloud is only available in one deployment model. (True | False)
3. Microsoft has data centers all over the globe, in all continents. (True | False)
4. You can assign a single Azure resource to multiple resource groups. (True | False)
5. Using your database as a service is considered a PaaS cloud service. (True | False)
6. Toast notifications are enabled by default in the Azure portal. (True | False)
7. What are the most common automation tools used with the Azure platform?

Further reading

- *What is Azure?* (https://azure.microsoft.com/en-us/overview/what-is-azure/)
- *Private Cloud vs Public Cloud* (http://www.ctrls.in/blog/private-cloud-vs-public-cloud/)

Understanding Azure Storage 2

This chapter introduces Microsoft Azure Storage, describing its importance, and the different types of Azure Storage. Then, you will learn about the different storage accounts and their different types, and in which scenarios they can be used. This is followed by an outline of the Azure services that you can use. Finally, we will cover the architecture of Azure Storage and look at what is going on behind the scenes.

The following topics will be covered in this chapter:

- Introduction to Microsoft Azure Storage
- Azure Storage types
- Azure Storage accounts
- Azure Storage services
- Azure Storage architecture

Introduction to Microsoft Azure Storage

Azure Storage is the bedrock of Microsoft's core storage solution offering in Azure. No matter what solution you are building for the cloud, you'll find find Azure Storage to be essential.

Azure Storage is a very scalable and highly available solution. You can store up to hundreds of terabytes of data. The data stored in Azure Storage is protected from corruption or loss because Azure Storage provides a highly available storage service that ensures that your data will be available, even if the primary storage server gets damaged.

Why use Azure Storage?

There are many reasons for using Azure Storage, which will be covered throughout this book. Some of them are listed here:

- **Global presence**: You can host your storage wherever you want in the available Azure regions, allowing you to provide applications close to your user base.
- **Redundancy and recovery**: Azure has a global presence that can be leveraged to maintain storage availability using data replication even if a disaster occurs in a specific region, which will be covered later in this chapter.
- **Many flavors**: Azure Storage has many flavors, based on resiliency, durability, connectivity, performance, and so on, which can be used according to your needs in different scenarios. This will be covered later in this chapter.
- **Pay as you go**: Pay as you go has always been one of the distinguished reasons for using the cloud generally. It is no surprise that Azure Storage supports this model as well.

Azure Storage types

Azure Storage has many types and even sub-types, to satisfy Azure service consumer needs.

The most common types can be classified based on the following factors:

- Durability (replication)
- Performance (standard versus premium)
- Persistency (persistent versus non-persistent)

Durability

One of the most popular questions about the cloud in general is *what if, for some reason, the SAN/servers that store my data are completely destroyed? How can I restore my data?*

The answer is very simple. Microsoft Azure Storage is durable and supports data replication; therefore, you can make sure your storage is highly available.

Replication ensures that your data is copied somewhere else, whether it is in the same data center, another data center, or even another region.

For more info about the SLA of Azure Storage, access the following link: https://azure.microsoft.com/en-us/support/legal/sla/storage/v1_2/.

Replication types

Microsoft Azure supports multiple options for data replication. You can use whatever suits your business, especially as every type has its own price.

In order to calculate your solution's cost, you can use the Azure pricing calculator, which can be reached via the following URL: https://azure.microsoft.com/en-us/pricing/calculator/.

Locally redundant storage

Locally redundant storage (LRS) replicates three copies of your data within the same data center. The write requests you do with your storage are not committed until they are replicated to all three copies, which means it replicates synchronously. Not only this, but it also makes sure that these three copies exist in different update domains and fault domains. More information about fault/update domains will be covered in Chapter 4, *Understanding Azure Virtual Machines*.

Drawbacks

The following points are the drawbacks for using LRS:

- The least durable option, as it replicates only within the same data center
- Your data will be lost if a catastrophic event, such as a volcanic eruption or flood, affects the data center

Advantages

The following points are the advantages of using LRS:

- It is the cheapest type compared to the other types
- It is the fastest type of data replication, offering the highest throughput, since it replicates within the same data center, mitigating the risk of data loss that would occur during data replication caused by a failure that occurred on the original data host
- It is the only available replication type that can be used with premium storage at the time of writing

Zone redundant storage

Zone redundant storage (**ZRS**) replicates three copies of data across two or three data centers within one of two regions asynchronously, plus the three copies of data stored within the same data center as the original source of the data.

Drawbacks

The following points are the drawbacks for using ZRS:

- This type can only be used for block blobs (one of the Azure services covered later in this chapter), and a standard storage account (general purpose standard storage accounts will be covered later in this chapter)
- Does not support metrics or logging
- Does not support conversion for other replication types, such as LRS, GRS, and vice versa
- If a disaster occurs, some data might be lost, because the data replicates to the other data centers asynchronously
- If a disaster occurs, there will be some delay in accessing your data until Microsoft failover to the secondary zone

Advantages

It provides higher durability and availability for data than LRS, as it not only replicates in the same data center, but also in other data centers.

Geo-redundant storage

Geo-redundant storage (GRS) replicates data not only within the same region, but also in other regions. Firstly, it makes three copies of the data within the same region synchronously, and then it makes another three copies of data in other regions asynchronously.

Drawbacks

- If a disaster occurs, some data might be lost, because the data replicates to the other regions asynchronously
- If a disaster occurs, there will be some delay in accessing your data until Microsoft initiates a failover to the secondary region

Advantages

- It provides the highest durability and availability, even if a disaster occurs in an entire region.
- Unlike ZRS, if the original source of data faces an outage, there will be no possibility of data loss if the other three copies that exist within the same region don't face an outage too, as it replicates synchronously within the same region.

Read-access geo-redundant storage

Read-access geo-redundant storage (RA-GRS) follows the same replication mechanism as GRS, in addition to read access on your replicated data in the other regions.

Drawback

If a disaster occurs, some data might be lost, because the data replicates to the other regions asynchronously.

Advantages

- It provides the highest durability and availability, even if a disaster occurs in a whole region
- If a disaster occurs, you still only have read access to the storage, but no write access until Microsoft initiates a failover to the secondary region
- The region with the read access can be used for data retrieval by the nearest offices to it without the need to go to another region to access the data; as a result, the data latency will decrease

Regarding replication between different regions, it will not work with just any two regions; the regions must be paired. For example, the West Europe region can replicate with North Europe, and not any other region.

For more information about paired regions, refer to the following article: `https://docs.microsoft.com/en-us/azure/best-practices-availability-paired-regions`.

Performance

As mentioned earlier, Azure provides services for all business types and needs. There are two types based on Azure Storage performance: standard and premium.

Standard storage

Standard storage is the most common type for all the VM sizes available in Azure. The standard storage type stores its data on non-SSD disks. It is commonly used with workloads where latency is not critical. Plus, it is low cost and has support for all Azure Storage services. It is also available in all regions.

Premium storage

Premium storage is designed for low latency applications, such as SQL Server, which needs intensive IOPs. Premium storage is stored on SSD disks. That is why it costs more than standard storage. Microsoft recommends using premium storage for better performance and higher availability.

Persistency

Another type of Azure Storage depends on data persistence. This means that data will be there or not after stopping and starting the VM within which your data exists.

Persistent storage

Persistent storage means that the data will be there after stopping and restarting the VM within which your data exists.

Non-persistent storage

Non-persistent storage means that the data will be gone after restarting the VM within which your data exists.

Azure storage accounts

An Azure storage account is a secure account that provides access to Azure storage services (which will be covered later in this chapter), and a unique namespace for storage resources.

During the creation of a new Azure storage account, you will have the option to choose one of three kinds of storage accounts:

- Storage (general purpose v1)
- StorageV2 (general purpose v2)
- Blob storage account

General-purpose storage account v1

A general-purpose storage account v1 gives you access to all Azure Storage services, such as blobs, tables, files, and queues, in a unified account. It has two performance tiers: standard and premium. This type is not the most cost-effective type of storage and it is the only type that still supports the classic Azure services and does not support the latest features.

Blob storage account

Unlike a general-purpose storage account, not all Azure Storage services are meant to be stored in a Blob storage account because they are dedicated to storing unstructured data. Therefore, a Blob storage service is the only type allowed to be accessed by a Blob storage account. However, it only supports blocks and appends blobs.

A Blob storage account has a usage pattern called access tiers, which determines how frequently you access your data and, based on that, what you will get billed. Currently, there are three types:

- Hot access tier
- Cool access tier
- Archive access tier

Hot access tier

With the hot access tier, objects will be accessed more frequently, so you will pay less for data access, but pay more for data size. This tier is commonly used for scenarios where you have data that has many read/write processes.

Cool access tier

With the cool access tier, objects will be accessed less frequently, so you will pay more for data access, but less for data size. This tier can be used as a backup solution since you will not be accessing this data frequently.

Archive access tier

This tier is meant for rarely accessed storage and it is the cheapest tier, as the terabyte would cost about $2.05 per month. Since this data will be offline, it can take up to 15 hours to move back to another tier to be able to access it again.

This tier is available at the blob level, not the storage account. It can be used as backup solution also but for long-term plans because you will barely access this data and in the meantime to benefit from its price or just storing your old data for compliance to the company's policies.

Premium access tier

At the time of writing, this tier is in preview. It provides high performance hardware and would fit very frequently accessed data with low latency. The data for this tier will be stored in SSDs and it supports the block Blob storage account type only as of now.

General-purpose storage account v2

This version combines the features of version 1 and the Blob storage account. In other words, this account will support the latest features for storage services, such as blobs, files, queues, and tables, in addition to the access tiers of Blob storage. It's recommended to make sure that your newly created storage account is v2.

Azure Storage account tips

The following tips will increase your knowledge about Azure Storage, and will definitely help you when you want to design a storage solution on Azure:

- You cannot switch between an Azure general-purpose storage account and an Azure Blob storage account, but you can upgrade a v1 general storage account to v2
- You can switch between access tiers with a Blob storage account and a v2 general storage account, but there is the possibility of additional charges being incurred
- A Blob storage account does not support the ZRS replication type at the time of writing
- Premium storage only supports locally redundant storage as a replication type at the time of writing
- Premium storage is not supported for a Blob storage account at the time of writing
- Azure supports up to 200 storage accounts per subscription by default
- A storage account can store data up to 500 TB
- If you are using REST APIs to connect to Azure Storage, you can secure the transfer by enabling that option during the creation of a storage account
- Only lowercase letters and numbers are supported for the name of a storage account
- Access tiers are not supported for premium storage accounts
- The archive access tier can only be set at blob level and not the account

Creating an Azure storage account

In this section, we will get create an Azure storage account. To do so, perform the following steps:

1. Open the Azure portal from here: `https://portal.azure.com/`.

2. Click on **All services** and a new blade will open. In the search bar, write `storage account`, as shown in the following screenshot:

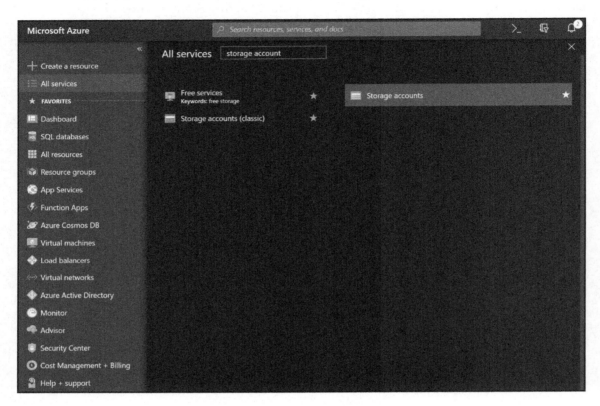

Figure 2.1: Searching for a storage account service

3. Click on **Storage accounts** and a new blade will open. Click on **Add**, as shown in the following screenshot:

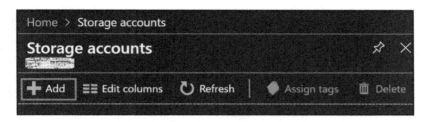

Figure 2.2: Adding a new storage account

4. A new blade will open. You need to fill in the fields and determine the following:
   - **Name**: The name of the storage account.
   - **Deployment model**: Select the deployment model that fits you. Only use **Classic** if you have other classic resources that need this resource to be classic too.
   - **Account kind**: Select the account kind that fulfill your needs.
   - **Location**: Select the nearest location to you.
   - **Replication**: Select the replication type according to the criticality of the services that will use this storage account. The higher the criticality, the higher the replication type you should go for.
   - **Performance**: Select **Premium** for services that will require fast data access and higher IOPs. Otherwise, select **Standard**.
   - **Access tier (default)**: Select the access tier that suits your case.
   - **Secure transfer required**: Either enable or disable this option. This option enhances the security of your storage account by only allowing requests to the storage account by a secure connection. For example, when calling REST APIs to access your storage accounts, you must connect using HTTPS. Any requests using HTTP will be rejected when it is enabled. When using the Azure file service, connection without encryption will fail, including scenarios using SMB 2.1, SMB 3.0 without encryption, and some flavors of the Linux SMB client. Because Azure Storage does not support HTTPS for custom domain names, this option is not applied when using a custom domain name.
   - **Subscription**: Select the subscription that will be charged for using this service.
   - **Resource group**: Either create a new one to logically gather this storage account in or select an existing one.

- **Configure virtual networks**: Enabling this setting will grant exclusive access to this storage account from the specified virtual network and subnets. This is providing that you can add more virtual networks and subnets after storage account creation. More information about this part will be covered in the next chapter:

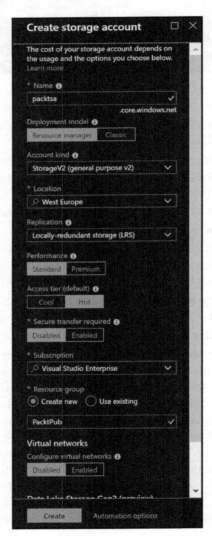

Figure 2.3: Creating a new storage account blade

5. Then, click on **Create** and wait for a moment until the account is created.
6. Once done, you can find your storage account in the **Storage accounts** blade:

Figure 2.4: Storage accounts blade

Azure Storage services

Azure Storage has multiple services that will fit most scenarios. At the moment, there are four types of Azure Storage services, which are as follows:

- Blob storage
- Table storage
- Queue storage
- File storage

Each of these services can be used for different scenarios, which we will cover in detail shortly.

Blob storage

Blob stands for **binary large object**. This type of service can store almost everything, since it stores unstructured data, such as documents, files, images, VHDs, and so on.

Using the Azure Blob storage service allows you to store everything that we have just mentioned, and you can access anything from anywhere using different access methods, such as URLs, REST APIs, or even one of the Azure SDK storage client libraries, which will be covered later in this chapter.

There are three types of Blob storage:

- **Block blobs**: They are an excellent choice to store media files, documents, backups, and so on. They are good for files that are read from A-Z (sequential reading).
- **Page blobs**: They support random access for files stored on them. That is why they are commonly used for storing VHDs of Azure virtual machines.
- **Append blobs**: They are similar to block blobs, but are commonly used to append operations. For example, each time a new block is created, it will be added to the end of the blob. One of the most common use cases within which append blobs can be used is logging, where you have multiple threads that need to be written to the same blob. This is an excellent solution that will help you to dump the logs in a fast and safe way.

Creating Blob storage

Let's see how we can create Blob storage, where everyone has read/write access to in the storage account that we created earlier in this chapter:

1. Navigate to the storage we created earlier in this chapter using the portal, as shown in the following screenshot:

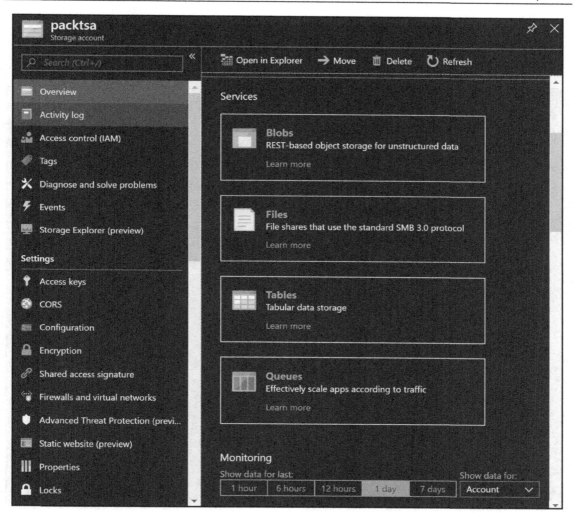

Figure 2.5: Azure Storage services overview

2. You can see all the storage services in the previous screenshot. To manage blobs, you have to click on **Blobs,** and a new blade will appear, as shown in the following screenshot:

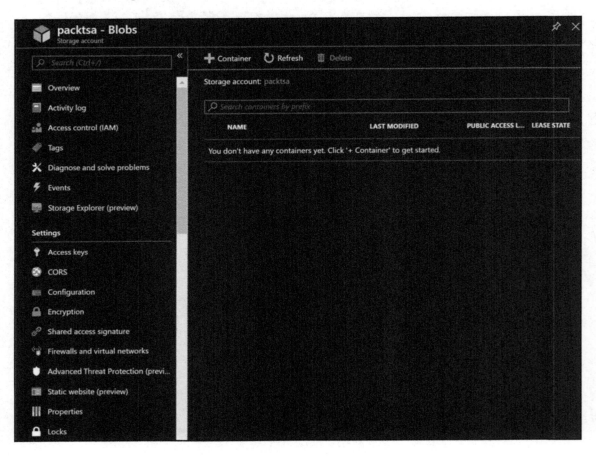

Figure 2.6: Azure blob service overview

3. In order to create a blob service, you have to create a container in which the blob service will be stored. To do this, you click on **Container** to create a new one. However, it is not a straightforward creation process, as you will be asked to specify a name and an access type, as shown in the following screenshot:

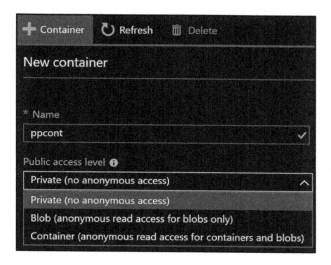

Figure 2.7: Creating a blob service

Here is a short description of the access types:

- **Private**: This option means that only the storage account owner has access to the blobs created within this container using the access key; therefore, you can grant access privileges to any other users
- **Blob**: This option means that the blobs created within this container will be accessed from outside by read permissions only
- **Container**: This option means that the blobs created within the container will be publicly available with read and write access

4. Since we want to create a blob service that everyone has read/write access to, we will choose **Public access level** as **Container (anonymous read access for containers and blobs)** and name it `ppcont`, as shown in the following screenshot:

Figure 2.8: Creating a blob service

 The access type of storage containers can be changed even after creation.

5. Once created, you can open the blob and start uploading your data to it, as shown in the following screenshot:

Figure 2.9: Uploading a .txt file to the blob

6. For further customization of the uploaded blob, click on **Advanced** and you will see options such as specifying the **Blob type**, **Block size**, to which folder it will upload the blob, and so on:

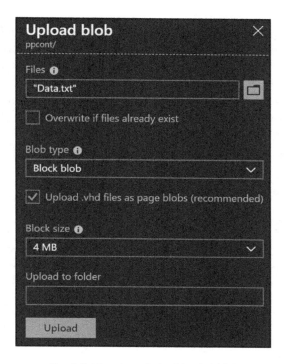

Figure 2.10: Advanced customization of the uploaded blob

Blob storage key points

The following tips should be considered, as they will help you when designing your storage solution using blob services:

- Blob storage supports both standards, but only page blobs support premium storage.
- Block blobs are named as such because files larger than 64 MB are uploaded as smaller blocks, and then get combined into one final blob.

- You cannot change the type of blob once it has been created.
- Block blobs are named as such because they provide random read/write access to 512-byte pages.
- Page blobs can store up to 8 TB.
- Storage containers built for Blob storage may only contain lowercase letters, hyphens, and numbers, and must begin with a letter or a number. However, the name cannot contain two consecutive hyphens. The name length can vary between three to 63 characters.
- The maximum number of blocks in a block blob or append blob is 50,000.
- The maximum size of the block in a block blob is 100 MB. As a result, a block blob can store data of up to 4.75 TB.
- The maximum size of the block in an append blob is 4 MB. As a result, an append blob can store data of up to 195 TB.

Table storage

High availability and scalability are key factors when you want to work with your storage, and that is exactly what is offered by Table storage. Table storage is a Microsoft NoSQL data store that can be used for a massive amount of semi-structured, non-relational data.

Data is stored in tables as a collection of entities, where entities are like rows, and each entity has a primary key and a set of properties, where a property is like a column.

The Table storage service is schema-less. Therefore, multiple entities in the same table may have different properties.

An entity has three properties:

- PartitionKey
- RowKey
- Timestamp

PartitionKey

The PartitionKey is a sequential range of entities that have the same key value. The way that tables are partitioned is to support load balancing across storage nodes, where table entities are organized by partition. It is considered the first part of an entity's primary key.

It may be a string value with a size of up to 1 KB, and every insert, update, or delete operation must be included in the PartitionKey property.

RowKey

RowKey is the second part of the entity's primary key. It is a unique identifier for the entity, and every entity in the table is uniquely identified by the combination of PartitionKey and RowKey.

Like PartitionKey, it is a string value that may be up to 1 KB, and every insert, update, or delete operation must be included in the RowKey property.

Timestamp

Timestamp is a datetime value, and it is kept on the server side to record when the last modification of the entity occurred.

Every time there is a modification of the entity, the timestamp value is increased. This value should not be set on insert or update operations.

Creating Table storage

Let's see how we can create Table storage in the storage account we created earlier in this chapter:

1. Navigate to the storage we created earlier in this chapter using the portal, as shown in the following screenshot:

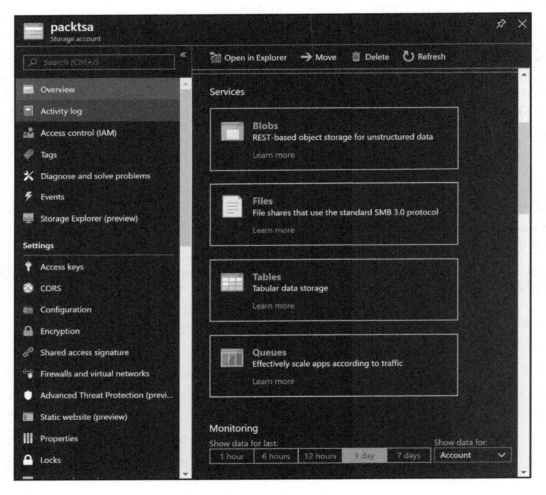

Figure 2.11: Azure Storage services overview

2. You can see all the storage services in the previous screenshot. To manage tables, you have to click on **Tables**, and a new blade will appear, as shown in the following screenshot:

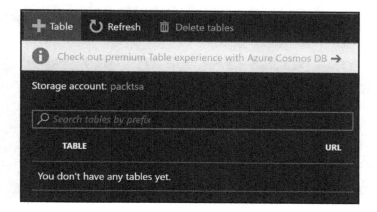

Figure 2.12: Azure Table service overview

3. In order to create a table service, just click on **Table** and specify the **Table name**, as shown in the following screenshot:

Figure 2.13: Azure Table service creation

4. Once done, you will see that the table has been created, as shown in the following screenshot:

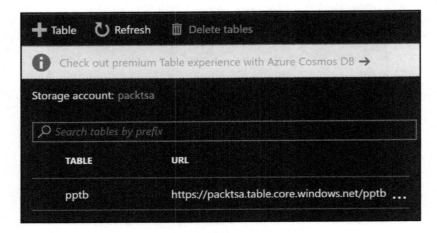

Figure 2.14: The created table

 For developers and administrators who are interested in learning how to access a created table and start working with it, you can check the following link: `https://docs.microsoft.com/en-us/azure/cosmos-db/table-storage-how-to-use-dotnet`.

Table storage key points

The following tips should be considered, as they will help you when designing your storage solution using the Table storage service:

- Table storage supports standard storage, but the premium table storage is available in Azure Cosmos DB.
- Table storage is significantly lower in cost than traditional SQL.
- The entity can have up to 252 custom properties, and three system properties (PartitionKey, RowKey, and Timestamp).
- The entity's property data cannot exceed 1 MB.

- Table names must follow the following rules:
  - They are case sensitive
  - They contain only alphanumeric characters, considering that they cannot begin with a numeric character
  - They cannot be redundant within the same storage account
  - You can name a table with another table name written in reverse
  - Their length varies between three and 63 characters

Queue storage

Queue storage is a storage service that is used to provide persistent and reliable messaging for application components.

Generally, it creates a list of messages that process asynchronously, following the **first-in, first-out (FIFO)** model. Not only this, but asynchronous tasks and building process workflows can be managed with Queue storage too.

One of the most common scenarios is passing messages from an Azure web role to an Azure worker role.

Queue storage is not the only messaging solution available with Azure; there are also Service Bus queues, which can be used for more advanced scenarios.

More information about the differences between Azure Queue storage and Azure Service Bus queues can be found via the following URL: https://docs.microsoft.com/en-us/azure/service-bus-messaging/service-bus-azure-and-service-bus-queues-compared-contrasted.

Creating Queue storage

Let's see how we can create Queue storage in the storage account that we created in the last chapter:

1. Navigate to the storage account we created earlier in this chapter using the portal, as shown in the following screenshot:

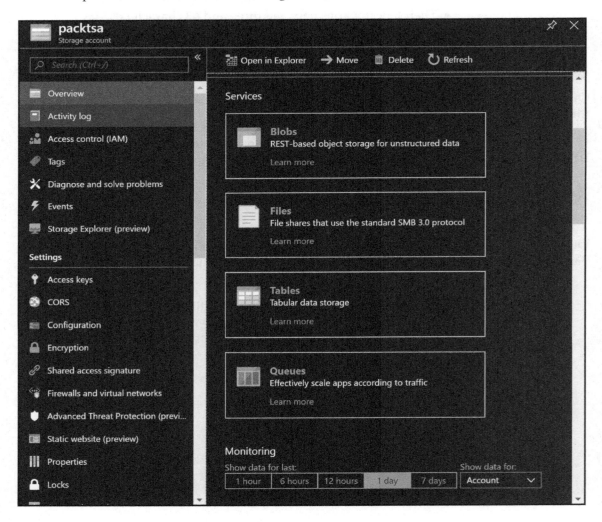

Figure 2.15: Azure Storage services

2. You can see all the storage services in the previous screenshot. To manage queues, you have to click on **Queues**, and a new blade will appear, as shown in the following screenshot:

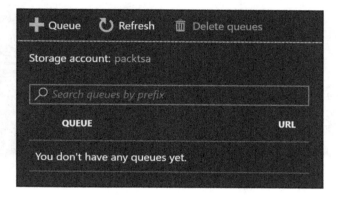

Figure 2.16: Azure Queue service overview

3. In order to create a queue service, just click on **Queue** and specify the **Queue name**, as shown in the following screenshot:

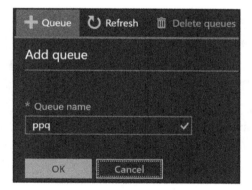

Figure 2.17: Azure queue service creation

4. Once done, you will see that the queue has been created, as shown in the following screenshot:

Figure 2.18: The created queue

 For developers who are interested in learning how to access a created queue and start working with it, you can checkout the following link: `https://docs.microsoft.com/en-us/azure/storage/queues/storage-dotnet-how-to-use-queues`.

Queue storage key points

The following tips should be considered, as they will help you when designing your storage solution using the queue service:

- Queue messages can be up to 64 KB in size. However, a queue can contain messages up to the limiting size of the storage account.
- The maximum lifetime of a message in a queue is 7 days.
- As mentioned previously, messages follow the FIFO order. However, they can be out of order if an application crash occurs, which is why it would be better to use Azure Service Bus queues for a scenario where the FIFO order is highly important.
- Messages can be scheduled for delivery later.
- A queue name may only contain lowercase letters, hyphens, and numbers, and must begin with a letter or number. It cannot contain two consecutive hyphens.
- Name length varies from between three and 63 characters.

File storage

The file storage service is the easiest and coolest service to work with. You can use it to create network file shares on Azure, and access them from anywhere in the world.

Server Message Block (SMB) and **Common Internet File System (CIFS)** are the only protocols that can be used to access these file shares.

As a result, multiple Azure VMs and on-premises machines can access the same file share and have read and write privileges on it. Azure file shares can be mounted to different operating systems, such as Windows, Linux, and even macOS, concurrently.

File storage advantages

The following are some of the benefits to be gained from using the file storage service:

- **Software as a Service (SaaS)**: The Azure file storage service is considered a SaaS service because you do not have to manage the hardware, operating system, patches, and so on. It is simply fully managed.
- **Shareability**: It can be shared across multiple machines, providing read and write privileges for all of those machines.
- **Automation**: It supports working with PowerShell and the Azure CLI, which can be used to create scripts to automate repetitive tasks with minimal administration.
- **Flexibility and high availability**: Using the Azure file storage service eliminates concerns regarding administration and outage issues that you face with traditional file servers.

Creating file storage

Let's see how we can create file storage in the storage account we created earlier in this chapter:

1. Navigate to the storage we created in the last chapter using the portal, as shown in the following screenshot:

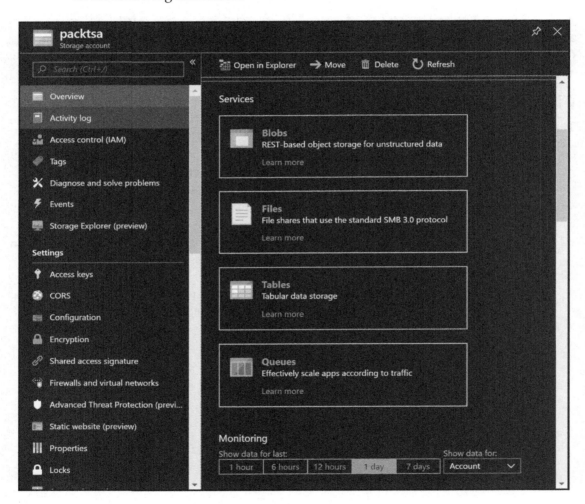

Figure 2.19: Azure Storage services

2. You can see all the storage services in the previous screenshot. To manage files, you have to click on **Files** and a new blade will appear, as shown in the following screenshot:

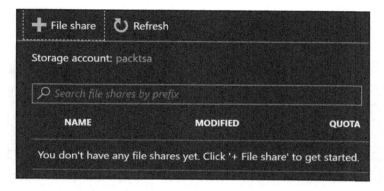

Figure 2.20: Azure file service overview

3. In order to create a file share, just click on **File share** and specify the file share **Name** and its **Quota**, considering that the quota is optional, as shown in the following screenshot:

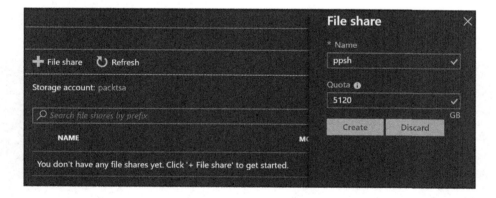

Figure 2.21: Azure file share creation

4. Once done, you will see that the file share has been created, as shown in the following screenshot. Considering that we never specified a quota, it used the maximum space the storage account can store; therefore, you have to design your file share properly, according to your needs and with the proper quota, to avoid any future issues caused by the space used. Also, you can change the quota even after file share creation:

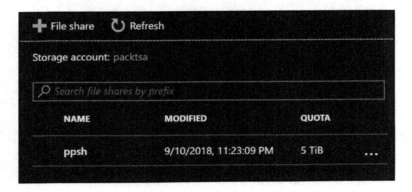

Figure 2.22: The created file share

5. You can map the file share to your Windows machine or Linux machine, adding directories within the file share, uploading data to it, and so on if you open it after creation, as shown in the following screenshot:

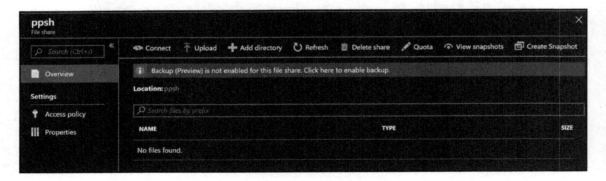

Figure 2.23: Overview of the created file share

6. To map the file share as a drive on your Windows or Linux machine, click on **Connect**, which will open a new blade, displaying the commands required to map it to your machine, as shown in the following screenshot:

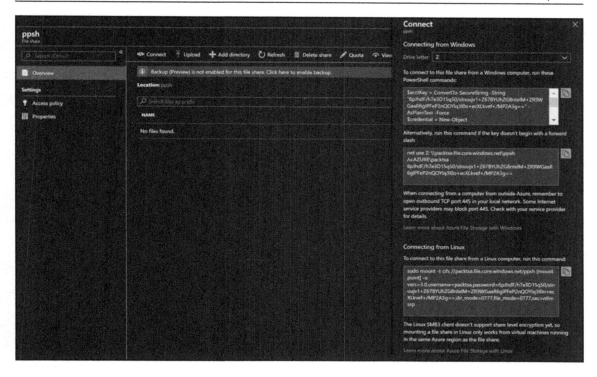

Figure 2.24: Connecting to your file share from your Windows or Linux machine

7. To upload files to it, click on **Upload** and browse for the desired file, as shown in the following screenshot:

Figure 2.25: Uploading a file to the file share

File storage key points

The following tips should be considered, as they will help you when designing your storage solution using the file service:

- Since SMB 2.1 does not support encryption, then only the VMs within the same region as the storage account will be able to access it if you are using SMB 2.1. As a result, you have to consider that you cannot access the read-only data available in another region if you are using RA-GRS as a replication type.
- Since SMB 3.0 supports encryption, you will be able to mount the file share to any VM around the globe, but port 445 must be opened.
- At the time of writing, only two versions of macOS were supported for Azure file shares (Sierra 10.12 and El Capitan 10.11).
- For better performance when working with Azure file shares on macOS, I recommend disabling SMB packet signing.
- The maximum size of a file share is 5 TB, considering that a file in the file share cannot exceed 1 TB.
- Every Azure file share supports up to 1,000 IOPS and 60 MB/s throughput.
- File share names can contain only lowercase letters, numbers, and hyphens, and must begin and end with a letter or number. The name cannot contain two consecutive hyphens.

Azure Storage architecture

Learning how to work with Azure Storage and how to design it to fit your solution is everyone's purpose, but learning what is going on behind the scenes and what every piece means is what makes you an expert.

Azure Storage is a distributed storage software stack built by Microsoft. The storage access architecture consists of the following three layers:

- Frontend layer
- Partition layer
- Stream layer

Frontend layer

The frontend layer is responsible for receiving incoming requests, their authentication, and authorization, and then delivers them to a partition server in the partition layer.

You may wonder, how does the frontend know which partition server to forward each request to? The answer is pretty easy, because the frontend caches a partition map.

And here, a new question will pop up: what is a partition map? It is responsible for keeping track of the partitions of the storage service being accessed, and which partition server controls access to each partition in the system.

Partition layer

The partition layer is responsible for partitioning all the data objects in the system. Not only that, it is also responsible for assigning the partitions to partition servers, plus load balancing the partitions across partition servers to meet the traffic needs of the storage services, considering that a single partition server can handle multiple partitions.

Stream layer

The stream layer or **Distributed and Replicated File System (DFS)** layer is the layer responsible for storing bits on the disk, and for data durability as it distributes and replicates data across many servers. All data stored in this layer is accessible from any partition server.

Sparse storage and TRIM in Azure

When you create a VHD on Azure to store your data on it, all the space you have chosen as a size for your VHD is completely allocated because Azure uses fixed-size VHDs. Therefore, you may wonder, will I really pay for the whole space even if I'm not using it, especially as it is not a dynamic disk but a fixed one?

Let's discuss this in more detail.

When you create a VHD, all the size is allocated, and that might trick you into using smaller VHDs to save costs, but actually that is not what really happens behind the scenes.

Azure uses sparse storage, which means no matter the size of the VHD you have created, you will only pay for what you have stored on the VHD. For example, you have a 1 TB VHD, but you have only 200 MB of storage stored on it. You will only pay for the 200 MB storage; therefore, as a best practice, you should create the VHD with the maximum storage to avoid any downtime later during the resizing process.

Microsoft does its best to charge you only for what you use; that's why Azure Storage supports TRIM, which means whenever you delete data from it, you no longer pay for the deleted storage.

 When you add a VHD, you should use a quick format for the disk, not the full format. Doing so will write the OS to the entire disk, which means you will have to pay for the entire disk. You should also consider not using defragmentation to avoid moving the disk blocks, which means greater costs will have to be paid.

Summary

In this chapter the information required to get your hands on Azure Storage has been covered. That includes identifying the different types of Azure Storage, storage services, which types of account services you should use, and so on. The chapter concluded with what's happening behind the scenes for Azure Storage to help you to fully understand it.

In the next chapter, we will cover Azure networking and how it works in Azure, the same as Azure Storage.

Questions

1. Premium storage is only available for the locally redundant storage replication type. (True | False)
2. Unlike all storage replication types, RA-GRS can be accessed whenever you want. (True | False)
3. You can downgrade from Storage Account v2 to Storage Account v1. (True | False)

4. Block blobs are the best Blob storage type for VHDs. (True | False)
5. Table storage is the best storage service for messaging. (True | False)
6. The stream layer is the layer responsible for storing bits on disk, and for data durability in Azure Storage. (True | False)

Further reading

- *Learning Microsoft Azure Storage* (https://www.packtpub.com/big-data-and-business-intelligence/learning-microsoft-azure-storage)
- Azure File Sync (https://4sysops.com/archives/install-azure-file-sync-afs/)
- Get started with Azure Table storage using .NET (https://docs.microsoft.com/en-us/azure/cosmos-db/table-storage-how-to-use-dotnet)
- Get started with Azure Queue storage using .NET (https://docs.microsoft.com/en-us/azure/storage/queues/storage-dotnet-how-to-use-queues)
- *Azure Storage security guide* (https://docs.microsoft.com/en-us/azure/storage/common/storage-security-guide)

Getting Familiar with Azure Virtual Networks

3

In this chapter, we will introduce Azure Virtual Networks, alongside a number of the Azure networking services that are commonly used. You will learn how to work with Azure Virtual Networks, subnets, public IP addresses, network security groups, service endpoints, and much more.

The following topics will be covered in this chapter:

- An introduction to Azure Virtual Networks
- Azure VNet related services
- Azure service endpoints

An introduction to Azure Virtual Networks

When the computer revolution took place, networks were a very important piece of the puzzle, letting computers communicate with each other.

Throughout the IT revolution, networks have been an indispensable part of every IT environment. It is no surprise that networking is a vital part of the cloud, for many reasons—from remote connections to your Azure VMs, to spanning your environment across on-premises networks and Azure. Networks are used with almost all Azure services, including (but not limited to) Azure VMs, Azure SQL Databases, Azure Web Apps, and so on.

What is Azure VNet?

Azure **Virtual Networks** (**VNets**) is one of the most commonly used Microsoft Azure networking services. Azure VNet is sort of like a LAN, within which you have address spaces that are divided into multiple subnets. Only private IP ranges can be used for the address spaces and their subnets.

Just like local area networks are used for machines and devices to communicate with each other, and to keep them isolated and secured in your on-premises(private data center), Microsoft introduced Azure VNets to do the same in the cloud.

Azure VNets is similar to that of a LAN, in which the address spaces can be divided into multiple subnets. Only private IP ranges can be used for the address spaces and their subnets.

The subnets within each address space are automatically routed. The address range of a subnet that is in use cannot be edited.

Why use Azure VNets?

Azure VNet has many capabilities, along with many benefits. Some of the benefits are as follows:

- **Isolation**: The dev/test environment in a VNet can be separated from the production environment which is from other virtual networks as VNet has the advantage of staying isolated from other virtual networks.
- **Communicating with other VNets**: By default, virtual networks are isolated from one another. However, you can reach resources in another VNet, because virtual networks can be connected to each other.

- **Broad network access**: By default, all Azure services have access to the internet, which means that you can access Azure services from wherever you want, using whatever method you want, as long as you have an internet connection.
- **Hybrid connectivity**: Azure VNet can be spanned to your data center. As a result, you will be able to connect to both your Azure resources and on-premises resources privately, without the need to connect via the internet.
- **Security**: You can secure your virtual networks by setting rules that determine which inbound and outbound traffic can be allowed to flow into and out of the VNet.

Creating an Azure VNet

To create an Azure VNet, perform the following steps:

1. Navigate to the Azure portal, and search for `virtual networks`; you will find two options, as follows:
    - **Virtual networks**: This is an Azure Resource Manager based service. This is the option that will be selected.
    - **Virtual networks (classic)**: This is an Azure Service Manager based service:

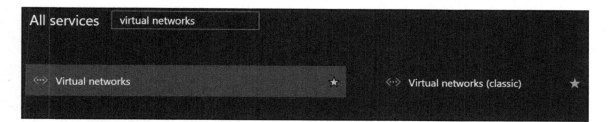

Figure 3.1: Searching for virtual networks

2. Click on **Virtual networks**, and a new blade will pop up, where you can check the virtual networks that you have (if any) or create a new one. To create a new one, click on **Add**, as shown in the following screenshot:

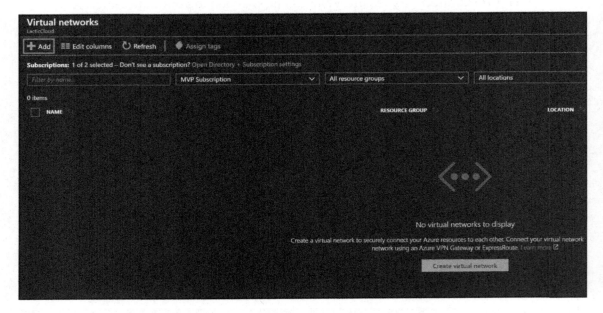

Figure 3.2: Virtual networks blade

3. Once you click on **Add**, a new blade will be opened, where you will have to specify the following:
   - **Name**: Specify a descriptive name for the VNet.
   - **Address space**: The VNet's address range in CIDR notation.
   - **Subscription**: Specify a subscription that will be charged for using this service.
   - **Resource group**: Either specify the resource group in which this resource will exist, or create a new one.
   - **Location**: Specify the nearest location.
   - **Subnet | Name**: Specify a descriptive subnet name.
   - **Subnet | Address range**: This is the subnet's address range, in CIDR notation. It must be contained by the address space of the VNet.
   - **DDoS protection**: This service offers protection from DDOS attacks. More information will be covered in the *Securing Azure VNets* section.

- **Service endpoint**: This can be used for securing the traffic between some Azure services in Microsoft's backbone network. More information will be covered in the *Securing Azure VNets* section.
- **Firewall**: Here, you choose whether you want to enable a firewall on the VNet. If you decide to enable it, you will be asked to provide a name, subnet address space, and public IP address for the firewall:

Figure 3.3: Creating a VNet

4. To create the VNet, click on **Create**, and it will be available for use within a few seconds.

Adding subnets to the VNet

There are two types of subnet in Azure VNet, as follows:

- **Subnet**: This is the normal form of subnets, which is the result of dividing the VNet
- **Gateway subnet**: This subnet is used by other networks as a mode of communication to communicate with each other

By default, you must specify at least one subnet when creating the VNet, as we illustrated earlier. However, later on, you might need to have other subnets; we'll cover that in the upcoming section.

Adding a normal subnet to the VNet

To add a subnet to the VNet, perform the following steps:

1. Navigate to the VNet that you created earlier, and then go to **Settings** | **Subnets**, as shown in the following screenshot:

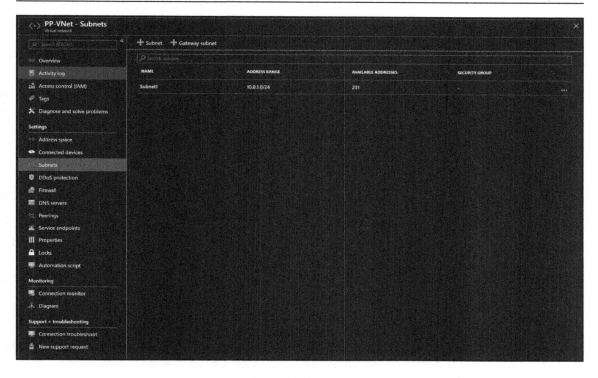

Figure 3.4: VNet subnets blade

2. Click on **Subnet**, and a new blade will be opened, where you will have to specify the following:
    - **Name**: The name of the subnet.
    - **Address range (CIDR block)**: The subnet's address range, in CIDR notation (it must be contained by the address space of the VNet).
    - **Network security group**: This works as a firewall, filtering traffic in and out of the network. More information about this topic will be covered in the *Securing Azure VNets* section.
    - **Route table**: You can expand the communication between multiple VNets by setting a route table, just like the routing tables in on-premises networks.
    - **Service endpoints**: As we mentioned earlier, this can be used to let some Azure services communicate in Microsoft's backbone network.

- **Subnet delegation**: You can enable private access between Azure services and the resources within this VNet. Such a delegation will allow the services to be deployed directly in the subnet:

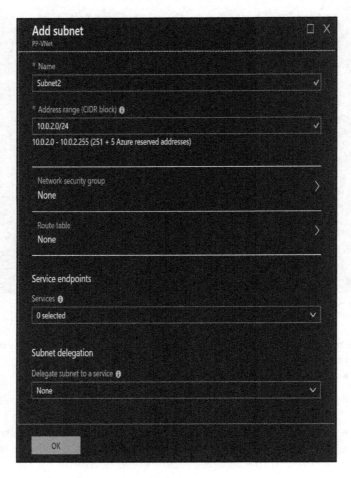

Figure 3.5: Adding a normal subnet

3. Once you are done, click on **OK** to add the subnet.

When specifying the subnet's address range, you may have noted that there are five reserved IPs. The first and the last IPs are reserved for protocol conformance, known as network and broadcast, in addition to three more IPs that are used for Azure services.

Adding a gateway subnet to the VNet

Adding a gateway subnet is almost the same as adding a normal subnet, with the following differences:

- You have to click on **Gateway subnet** instead of **Subnet**.
- This kind of subnet does not support associating network security groups to it.
- The name of the subnet is **GatewaySubnet** by default, and cannot be edited.
- Every VNet can have only one gateway subnet:

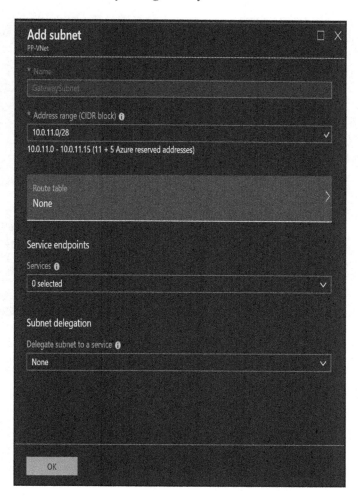

Figure 3.6: Adding a gateway subnet

Adding an address space to the Azure VNet

You can add other address spaces to the VNet, and later, those address spaces can be divided into subnets. To add another address space, follow these steps:

1. Navigate to the VNet blade that you created earlier.
2. Under **Settings | Address space**, you can view the current address spaces of the VNet, as shown in the following screenshot:

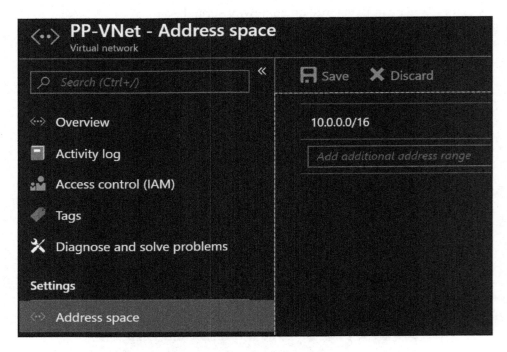

Figure 3.7: Viewing the address spaces of the VNet

3. In the field **Add additional address range**, you can add the new address space, then click on **Save**, as shown in the following screenshot:

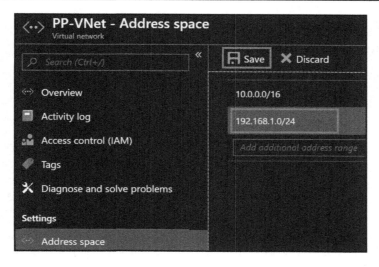

Figure 3.8: Adding an address space to a VNet

 For the key points to be remembered while building your VNet, you can refer to the first chapter of the book *Hands-On Networking with Azure*, written by me and published by Packt: `https://www.packtpub.com/ virtualization-and-cloud/hands-networking-azure`.

Azure VNet related services

There are many Azure networking services related to Azure VNets, such as public IPs, **network interface cards** (**NICs**), and so on. In this section, we will look into each of these services.

Public IPs

When you get familiar with Azure services, you will note that there are many Azure services that require public IPs, such as Azure VMs, Azure SQL servers, Azure load balancers, and much more. Fortunately, Microsoft provides public IPs that can be used.

For a while you got to create every public IP address without knowing which IP address would be assigned to you, but Azure recently released a new service, called public IP prefixes, that helps you to create a set of public IPs that are reserved for you, from which you can select which public IP address you want to assign to your Azure service.

Creating a public IP address

To create a public IP address, follow these steps:

1. Navigate to the Azure portal and search for `Public IP addresses`, as shown in the following screenshot:

Figure 3.9: Searching for public IP addresses

2. A new blade will pop up, where you can view the created public IP addresses (if any) and add new public IP address. To add a new one, click on **Add**, as shown in the following screenshot:

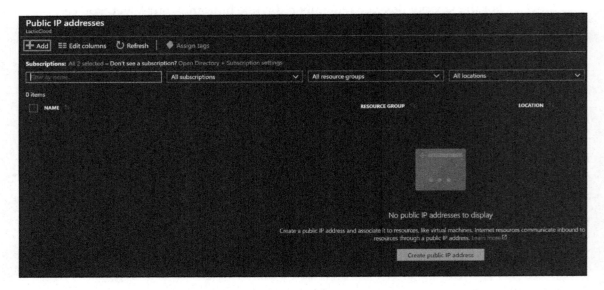

Figure 3.10: Public IP addresses blade

3. A new blade will be opened, where you will have to specify the following:
    - **Name**: Specify a descriptive name for the public IP address.
    - **SKU**: Specify the tier of the public IP address:
        - **Basic**: This type has been around since the launch of public IP addresses in Azure.
        - **Standard**: This is a new SKU that only supports IPv4. Inbound traffic of this IP must be allowed in the NSG to be able to function properly, and zone-redundant.
    - **IP Version**: Specify the version of IP address that you want to use.
    - **IP address assignment**: Specify the allocation method, whether static or dynamic.
    - **Idle timeout (minutes)**: Specify the period for which it will keep a TCP or HTTP connection open, without relying on clients to send keep-alive messages.
    - **DNS name label**: A record that starts with the specified label and resolves to this public IP address will be registered with the Azure-provided DNS servers.
    - **Create an IPv6 address**: You can add an additional IPv6 to the same public IP address.
    - **Subscription**: Specify the subscription that will be charged for using this IP address.

- **Resource group**: Either specify a resource group in which this resource will exist, or create a new one.
- **Location**: Specify the location nearest to you:

Figure 3.11: Creating a new public IP address

4. Finally, you can click on **Create** to create the public IP address.

Creating a public IP prefix

At the time of writing this book, the feature in this section was available for public preview. To create a public IP prefix, follow these steps:

1. Navigate to the Azure portal and search for `public ip prefixes`:

Figure 3.12: Searching for public IP prefixes

2. A new blade will be opened, where you can view the created public IP prefixes (if any). To add a new public IP prefix, click on **Add**, as shown in the following screenshot:

Figure 3.13: Public IP Prefixes blade

3. When you click on **Add**, a new blade will be opened where you have to specify the following:

      - **Subscription**: Specify the subscription that will be charged for using this service.
      - **Resource group**: Either specify the resource group in which this resource will exist, or create a new one.
      - **Name**: Specify a descriptive name for the set of public IPs.
      - **Region**: Specify the region nearest to your services.
      - **Prefix size**: Specify the prefix size that will fulfill your needs:

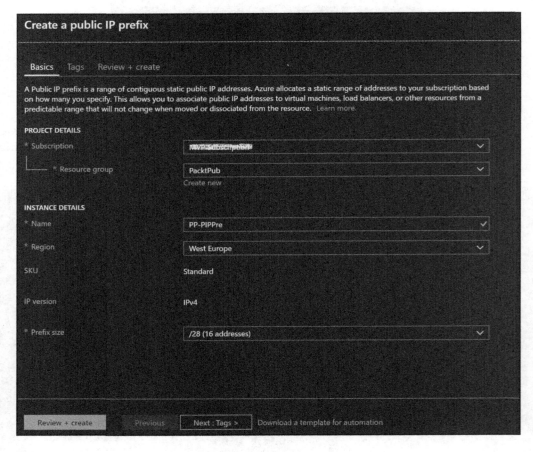

Figure 3.14: Public IP prefix creation blade

4. Then, you can click on **Next: Tags >** button if you want to add tags for the public IP prefix, so you can categorize resources and view consolidated billing; or, click on **Review + create** if you do not want to add tags. If so, your input will be validated and a summary will be displayed, as shown in the following screenshot:

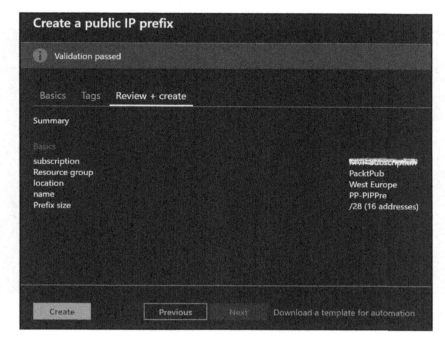

Figure 3.15: Summary of the public IP prefix configuration

5. Once the validation is complete (and once you have checked that the input you have provided is correct, according to the summary), you can click on **Create** to create the public IP prefix.

NICs

NICs are a vital component of one of the most important Azure services: Azure VMs.

To create an NIC, follow these steps:

1. Navigate to the Azure portal and search for `Network interfaces`.
2. Click on it and a new blade will be opened, where you can view the previously created NICs (if any) and add a new NIC by clicking on **Add**, as shown in the following screenshot:

Figure 3.16: Network interfaces blade

3. Once you have clicked on **Add**, a new blade will be opened, where you will have to specify the following:
   - **Name**: Specify a descriptive name for the NIC.
   - **Virtual network**: Specify which VNet you want to assign this NIC to.
   - **Subnet**: Specify which subnet in the VNet you want to assign this NIC to.
   - **Private IP address assignment**: Specify the allocation method of the private IP address that will be assigned to the NIC (**Dynamic** or **Static**).
   - **Network security group**: Specify a network security group for the NIC, if you wish. More information about network security groups will be covered later, in the section *Securing Azure VNets*.
   - **Private IP address (IPv6)**: You can add a private IPv6 to the same NIC.

- **Subscription**: Specify the subscription that will be charged for using this service.
- **Resource group**: Either specify a resource group in which this resource will exist, or create a new one.
- **Location**: Specify the region nearest to your services:

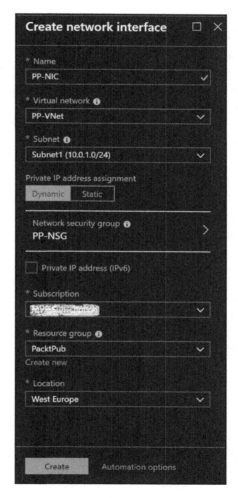

Figure 3.17: Creating an NIC

4. Once you are done, click on **Create**.

Whenever we buy a new service, the most important aspect that we look into is security. In this `article` which is an excerpt from the book, *Hands-On Networking with Azure*, authored by me and published by Packt, you will find a detailed study on *Network Security Groups* that has total control over the flow of traffic.

Azure service endpoints

Azure VNet service endpoints create a direct connection to the service, with which you want to communicate, via the VNet where you have enabled service endpoints. Doing so will ensure that all of the traffic between your data center and Azure service is performed via the Microsoft network backbone.

At the time of writing this book, this feature was generally available for the following Azure services:

- Azure Storage
- Azure SQL Databases
- Azure Database for PostgreSQL server
- Azure Database for MySQL Server
- Azure Cosmos DB
- Azure Key Vault

It is in preview for the following Azure services:

- Azure SQL Data Warehouse
- Azure Service Bus
- Azure Event Hubs

Summary

So far, we have covered the most commonly used Azure networking services, such as Azure VNets, subnets, NSGs, NICs, service endpoints, and so on. These services are the core services of Azure networking. Therefore, you will need this knowledge in the coming chapter, in order to get a full picture of how Azure services work with each other.

In the next chapter, we will cover Azure VMs. You will learn how to create and manage VMs in Azure. To do so, you will need the knowledge that you have gained from the previous chapters.

Questions

1. You can create a VNet with zero subnets. (True | False)
2. You can create only one gateway subnet per VNet. (True | False)
3. The public IP address can operate as IPv4 and IPv6 at the same time. (True | False)
4. For each subnet that you create, there are five reserved IP addresses. (True | False)

Further reading

- *Securing Azure VNets* (https://hub.packtpub.com/secure-azure-virtual-network/)
- *Hands-On Networking with Azure* (https://www.packtpub.com/virtualization-and-cloud/hands-networking-azure)
- *Configure Azure Storage Firewalls and Virtual Networks* (https://docs.microsoft.com/en-us/azure/storage/common/storage-network-security)
- *What is Azure Firewall?* (https://docs.microsoft.com/en-us/azure/firewall/overview)
- *Azure DDoS Protection Standard overview* (https://docs.microsoft.com/en-us/azure/virtual-network/ddos-protection-overview)

Understanding Azure Virtual Machines

4

In this chapter, we will cover one of the most popular Azure services: Azure virtual machines. We will introduce you to Azure VMs and their types. You will learn how to create Azure VMs, and how they relate to Azure Storage and networks.

The following topics will be covered in this chapter:

- Introducing Azure virtual machines
- Creating an Azure virtual machine
- Azure virtual machine storage
- Azure virtual machine networking

Introducing Azure virtual machines

Azure **virtual machines** (**VMs**) comprise the most well-known and usable service available in Azure, as well as the oldest. Azure virtual machines provides deployment of different flavors of Windows and Linux VMs.

Azure VMs provide you with full control over the configuration and management of the VM. Management refers to installing software, patching, and even maintaining the VM.

Azure VM statuses

Fortunately, Microsoft bills VMs per minute, not per hour; therefore, when you use a VM for 30 minutes, you will only be charged for 30 minutes. Also, when the VM is not running, you will not be charged for the computing resources (CPU and memory); however, you will be charged for the VM storage. Let's discuss the VM states in more detail:

State	Description
Running	The VM is running, and you will get charged for the usage, as usual
Stopped	The VM has been shut down from inside the OS, but you can still get charged for the VM, as it is still deployed to the same physical host, and the resources are still reserved for it
Stopped (deallocated)	The VM was stopped by the stop button on the VM blade, via the Azure portal

You can make use of the Reserved Instances payment model for Azure VMs. This model enables you to reserve a VM for one, two, or three years, and that provides a high cost reduction, as compared to the pay as you go model. The cost savings can be up to 82%. For more information about Reserved Instances, browse to https://azure.microsoft.com/en-us/pricing/reserved-vm-instances/.

Azure VM service level agreements

At the time of writing this book, Microsoft had three **service level agreements (SLAs)** for Azure VMs, as follows:

- Two or more VMs within the same Availability Set have 99.95% availability
- Using a single VM that uses premium storage will provide at least 99.9% availability
- Two or more VMs within the same Availability Zone have 99.99% availability

In order to understand the difference between Availability Sets and Availability Zones, you will have to understand the following terminologies:

- **Fault domain**: A group of resources that could fail at the same time. For example, if all of the resources are all running on a single rack, sharing the same power source and physical network switch then, they could fail.
- **Update domain**: A group of resources that can be updated simultaneously during system upgrades. For example, when Microsoft decides to update/upgrade the hosts on which the VMs run in groups of hosts and not for all of the hosts at the same time, each group is considered an update domain.

Now, you will be able to understand the difference between Availability Set and Availability Zone:

- **Availability Set**: This provides high availability for the VMs by setting VMs within different update and fault domains in the same data center.
- **Availability Zone**: This does the same thing as an Availability Set, except that it spans across multiple data centers in the same region. Therefore, if one of the data centers faces an outage, you will still have at least one VM running on another data center in the same region.

 To keep up to date with Microsoft SLAs for Azure VMs, keep your eye on https://azure.microsoft.com/en-us/support/legal/sla/virtual-machines/v1_8/.

Azure VM series

Azure VMs have multiple series, in order to fit into different cases and scenarios, as follows:

- **A-Series**: This series is most commonly used in dev/test scenarios, and it has been around since the early days of Azure VMs
- **B-Series**: This series provides the lowest cost of any existing size with flexible CPU usage; it mainly targets web servers, small databases, and dev/test environments
- **D-Series**: This series has fast CPU and SSD disks, and it is most commonly used in general purpose computing, such as relational databases and every application that requires high IOPS
- **E-Series**: This series is meant for heavy in-memory applications that require high memory-to-core ratios, such as the relational database servers that need medium to large caches
- **F-Series**: This series targets the applications that require intensive computing power, such as web servers
- **G-Series**: This series targets applications that require high memory and fast storage, such as ERP and SAP solutions
- **H-Series**: This series has very high computing capabilities, and it might fit scenarios that require that high performance, such as analytics
- **L-Series**: This series is dedicated to applications that require low latency, such as NoSQL databases, high throughput, high IOPS, and large disks
- **N-Series**: This series has high GPU capabilities, and can fit in scenarios such as video editing, graphical rendering, and so on
- **M-Series**: This series provides the biggest VM sizes in Azure, as of the time of writing this book; this series is a better fit for large in-memory workloads, such as SAP HANA and SQL Hekaton

For further information about the Azure VM series (and the new series that will be added), you can check https://azure.microsoft.com/en-us/ pricing/details/virtual-machines/series/.

Creating an Azure VM

Creating an Azure VM is a very straightforward process; all you have to do is follow these steps:

1. Open the Azure portal and navigate to **Virtual machines**, as shown in the following screenshot:

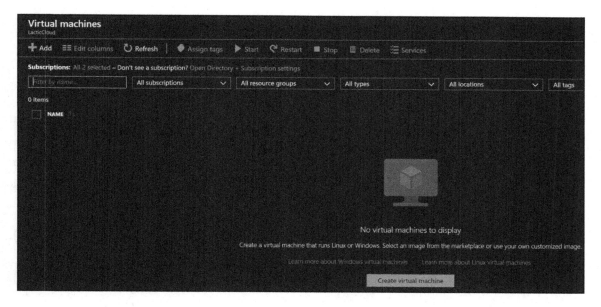

2. Click on **Add**, and a new blade will be opened, where you will have to specify some common requirements with which you should be familiar, such as the following:
    - **Subscription**: The subscription that will be charged for using this service
    - **Resource group**: The resource group in which Azure VM will exist as a resource
    - **Name**: The name of the VM
    - **Region**: Select the nearest region to you or to the services that would work with this VM.

- **Availability options**: Azure offers a range of options for managing the availability and resiliency of your applications. You can select any of the following three options, according to how critical the applications that you will operate in the VMs are:
  - **No infrastructure redundancy required**: No high availability will be provided, unless it will be using premium storage.
  - **Availability Zone**
  - **Availability Set**
- **Image**: Select the base OS for this VM.
- **Size**: Select a VM size that will fulfill the needs of the application that you will run on this VM (you can change the size later):

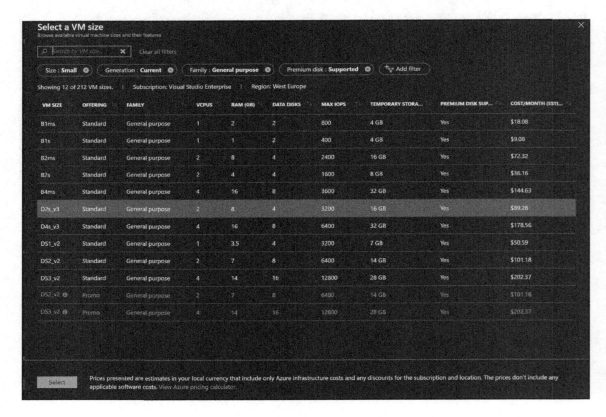

- **Administrator account**: Specify a username and a password for the VM.

- **Inbound port rules**: Specify whether you want to allow access via specific ports. If you have NSG, you can select **None** and specify the NSG in the coming steps.
- **Save money**: If you have a Windows Server license that supports the Hybrid Use benefit, you can use it to save up to 49% of the VM charges:

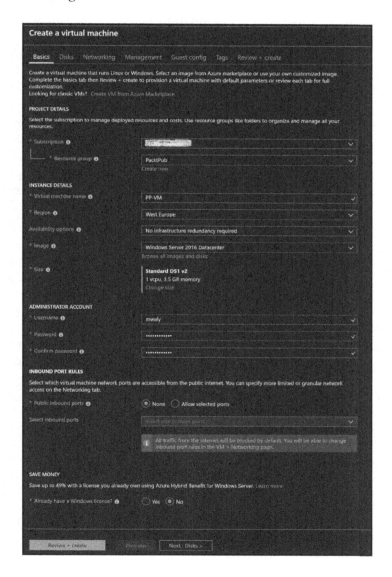

For more information about the Azure Hybrid Benefit, you can check https://docs.microsoft.com/en-us/azure/virtual-machines/windows/hybrid-use-benefit-licensing.

3. Then, you can click on **Review + create**, which will navigate you directly to the **Summary** blade, and will assign the default configurations for the VM; or, you can continue to work on customizing the VM, by clicking on **Next : Disks >**.

4. In the **Disks** blade, you need to specify the following:
   - **OS disk type**: There are three disk types that you can use, as follows:
     - **Standard HDD**: This type is backed by magnetic drives, and is preferable for applications where data is accessed infrequently.
     - **Standard SSD**: This type is meant for the same workloads as the standard HDD, but it provides better performance.
     - **Premium storage**: This type is backed by SSD disks that offer consistent, low-latency performance. It would be a good choice for I/O-intensive workloads.
   - **Use unmanaged disks**: If you select using unmanaged disks, you will be asked to specify a storage account to store the VHD/s of the VM, and you will be responsible for managing and monitoring the storage account, especially regarding the limits of the data size and the IOPS allowed in the storage account. On the other hand, if you decide to use managed disks, you will be offered the best performance, reliability, scalability, and access control for the disk.
   - **Data disks**: You can create a new data disk to attach to the VM, or you can attach an existing one; you can even skip it and add the data disks later:

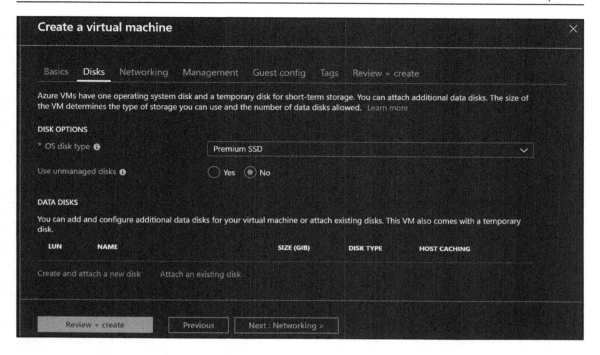

5. To proceed to the next phase of configuring networking for the VM, click on **Next : Networking >**, and you will be navigated to another blade, where you can specify the following:
    - **Virtual network**: You can create a new one or select an existing one.
    - **Subnet**: If you selected an existing one, you can select which subnet to use in this VNet; if you created a new one, it will be named **default**.
    - **Public IP**: Specify a public IP address for the VM to be accessed via the internet. You can create a new one or select an existing one.
    - **Configure network security group**: If you want to create a new one for the VM, you can select **Basic** and specify the allowed ports. If you already have one, you can select **Advanced** and specify the NSG that you want to select.

- **Accelerated networking**: If the VM size that you selected supports this feature, I recommend turning it on. It will provide low latency and high throughput to the VM NIC:

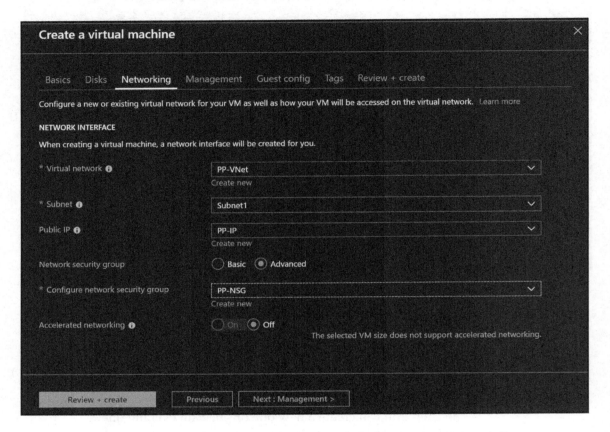

6. Next step is to configure the management options for the VM, as follows:
    - **Boot diagnostics**: Enable this if you wish to capture the serial console output and screenshots of the virtual machine running on a host, to help diagnose start up issues.
    - **OS guest diagnostics**: Enable this if you wish to get metrics for the VM every minute, which can be used to create alerts and stay informed on your applications.
    - **Diagnostics storage account**: If you have enabled any of the previous diagnostics, you will have to specify a storage account to store these diagnostics, so that you can analyze them with your own tools.

- **Managed service identity**: Enabling this service will register the VM with active directory, allowing you to control its access to storage accounts and other services. More information about Active Directory will be covered in `Chapter 9`, *Understanding Azure Active Directory*.
- **Enable auto-shutdown**: Enable this option if you use the VMs for a specific period of time every day. You can determine when it can be turned off automatically.
- **Enable backup**: You can make use of Azure Backup to protect your VM against accidental deletion and corruption. More information about Azure Backup will be covered in `Chapter 11`, *Data Protection and Business Continuity using OMS*:

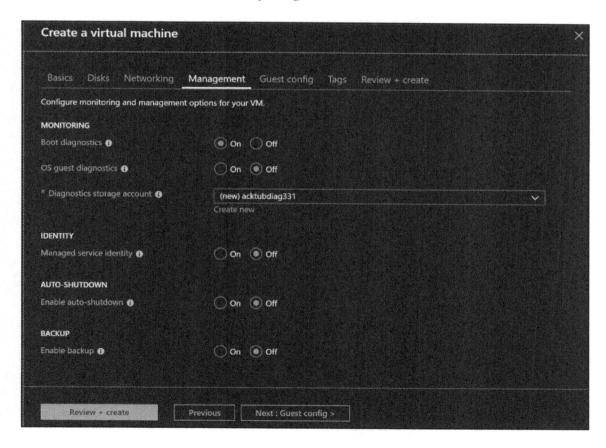

7. The next step will involve some guest configuration:
    - You can add some features to the VM, such as configuration management, antivirus protection, and so on. Click on **Select an extension to install**, which will open a new blade that shows all of the extensions that you can select from, as shown in the following screenshot:

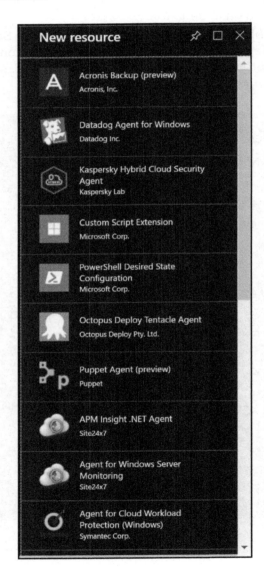

- CLOUD INIT is widely used approach for customizing a Linux based VM when it boots for the first time. It can be used to install packages, write files, or configure users and security. Therefore, if you have selected a Linux OS image, you should expect the following box, in which to specify your configuration:

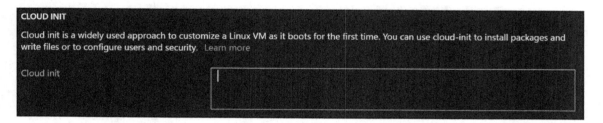

- With these configurations, you can get a ready to go VM without the need to install and configure some elements after getting it up and running:

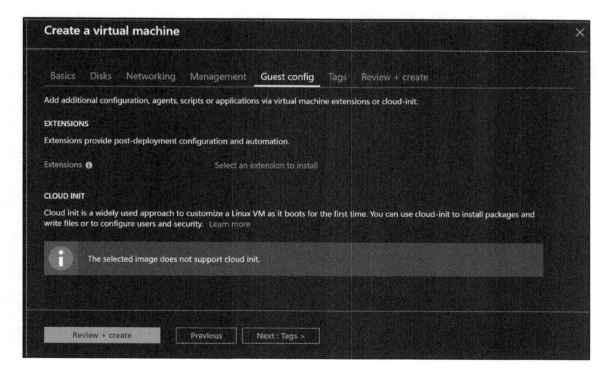

8. Next, you can add tags to the VM, if you wish. The tags are meant to provide metadata about the created resources, logically organizing them, which would be helpful for management and billing. The tags consist of a key and a value. For example, the key could be a department and the value could be the sales:

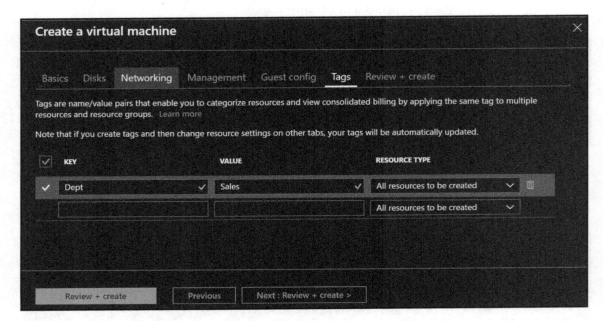

9. Finally, the configuration that you have specified will be validated and summarized, so that you can check what you have specified so far; once you are ready, click on **Create** to start deploying the VM:

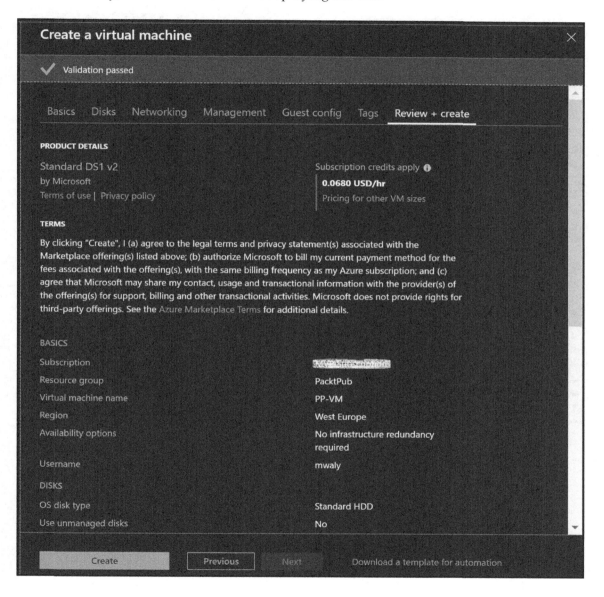

10. Once the VM is deployed, you can navigate to the **Virtual machines** blade and open it, as shown in the following screenshot:

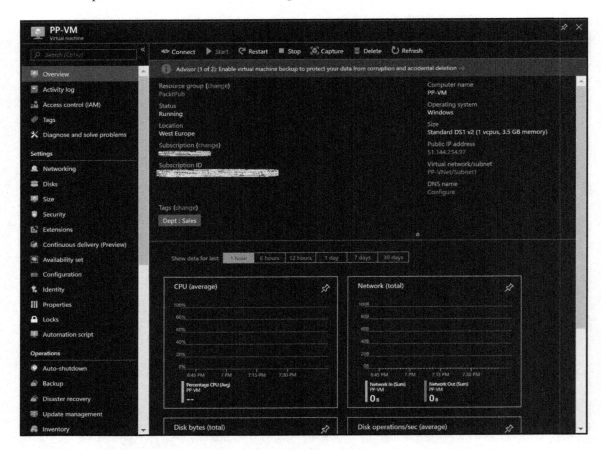

11. You can connect to the VM by clicking on **Connect**, which will download a preconfigured RDP file; once you open it, you will be asked to enter the VM credentials, as shown in the following screenshot:

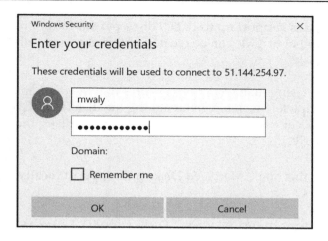

Azure VM storage

As we mentioned earlier, Azure VMs depend on Azure Storage to function properly. Now, let's go through some storage considerations for Azure VMs, in order to create a better design for your environment.

Managed versus unmanaged disks

As we mentioned earlier, managed disks save effort, and they support both premium storage and standard storage.

Managed Disks-key points

Let's cover some of the key points of Managed Disks, which may influence your design, and even your choice of using them:

- **Simplicity**: Using Managed Disks will eliminate many concerns when it comes to storage design, because you do not have to consider the limitations of the storage account, such as IOPS. For example, if you have multiple VMs running, and their disks are assigned to the same storage account, you might face some performance issues, because the VM disks have exceeded the IOPS limitations.

Managed Disks support up to 10,000 disks per subscription, which means that a massive number of VMs can be created within the same subscription when using Managed Disks.

- **Reliability**: Using managed disks ensures that the disks in an availability set in a VM are completely isolated, by assigning the disks to different storage scale units; whenever a failure occurs in one of the VM disks, the other VM disks still work properly.

At the time of writing this book, Managed Disks only support **locally redundant storage (LRS)** replication types.

- **Azure Backup support**: Managed Disks support Azure backup, and this is very important to consider, because if the data center in which your storage exists gets damaged, you must have a backup of your storage in another region.
- **Snapshot support**: Managed disks support snapshots, which are read-only copies of Managed Disks; therefore, they can be used as a backup method. The storage for which snapshots are created gets charged independently, based on its size.
- **Image support**: When you want to create an image from a Sysprep VM, you can capture an image of all of its Managed Disks. Then, it can be used later, as a template to create other VMs.
- **Costs**: When using Azure, you have to consider that everything comes with a price. Most of the time, it is not expensive; however, when you are using Managed Disks, you must consider the storage type, disk size, and so on, because that adds more credit.

A snapshot can only be taken for one disk at a time; so, if you have multiple disks that use one of the RAID techniques, you cannot restore the disks again with the same state, because Azure snapshots have no awareness of that.

Images and snapshots are completely different. An image is a like a VM template that can be used to recreate other VMs with the same specifications, and that includes the disks attached to it. However, snapshots are a picture of a point in time in one disk. For example, a snapshot of a disk can be considered a backup for a disk, and can be reused later, for other VMs.

To calculate the expected credits for using Managed Disks with regard to your environment's size, you can refer to the pricing calculator at `https://azure.microsoft.com/en-us/pricing/calculator/`; for further information about pricing and billing for Azure Managed Disks, you can check `https://docs.microsoft.com/en-us/azure/storage/storage-managed-disks-overview#pricing-and-billing`.

VM disks

Whenever you create a VM, there will be an OS disk attached to it, as well as a data disk (if you attached it). So, let's look at the types of VM disks, as follows:

- **OS disk**: The disk on which the operating system files exist, which is the `C:` drive in Windows by default, and `dev/sda` for Linux. The OS disk size can be up to 2 TB.
- **Temporary disk**: This disk exists in any VM by default, but, as the name suggests, it is temporary, which means it is non-persistent; in other words, whenever your VM is turned off, the data will be lost. This disk provides temporary storage, and it uses the `D:` drive by default in Windows, and `/dev/sdb1` in Linux. The temporary storage exists in the physical host of the VM; however, due to a failure in that physical host and if the VM is moved to any other host at any time, your data will be lost. Also, the temporary disk size varies, based on the VM size. In addition to this, when you are using temporary storage, no charges will be incurred. If you restart the VM via Windows, you will not lose the data that exists in the temporary storage disk; otherwise you will lose it if any downtime occurs for what so ever reason.
- **Data disk**: Data disks are used to store permanent data, which means they are persistent. For example, you can save your SQL database, or any other application data. As of the time of writing this book, a data disk's maximum size is almost 4 TB for unmanaged disks, and 32 TB for managed disks; you can add more than one data disk to a VM, according to the VM's size.

One of the most commonly used cases for temporary disks is storing the paging files; after all, every time the VM starts up, the paging file will be created in the temporary storage.

Microsoft has made a good comparison of the Azure Premium disk versus the Azure Standard disks, as shown in the following table:

	Azure Premium disk	Azure Standard SSD disk	Azure Standard HDD disk
Disk type	Solid State Drives (SSD)	SSD	Hard Disk Drives (HDD)
Overview	SSD-based, high-performance, low-latency disk support for VMs running IO-intensive workloads or hosting mission critical production environment.	More consistent performance and reliability than HDD. Optimized for low-IOPS workloads.	HDD-based, cost-effective disk support for infrequent access.
Scenario	Production and performance-sensitive workloads.	Web servers, lightly used enterprise applications, and dev/test.	Backup, non-critical, infrequent access.
Disk size	P4: 32 GB (managed disks only) P6: 64 GB (managed disks only) P10: 128 GB P15: 256 GB (managed disks only) P20: 512 GB P30: 1,024 GB P40: 2,048 GB P50: 4,095 GB P60: 8,192 GB * (8 TB) P70: 16,384 GB * (16 TB) P80: 32,767 GB * (32 TB)	Managed disks only: E10: 128 GB E15: 256 GB E20: 512 GB E30: 1,024 GB E40: 2,048 GB E50: 4,095 GB E60: 8,192 GB * (8 TB) E70: 16,384 GB * (16 TB) E80: 32,767 GB * (32 TB)	Unmanaged disks: 1 GB - 4 TB (4095 GB) Managed disks: S4: 32 GB S6: 64 GB S10: 128 GB S15: 256 GB S20: 512 GB S30: 1,024 GB S40: 2,048 GB S50: 4,095 GB S60: 8,192 GB * (8 TB) S70: 16,384 GB * (16 TB) S80: 32,384 GB * (32 TB)
Max throughput per disk	P4: 25 MB/s P6: 50 MB/s P10: 100 MB/s P15: 200 MB/s P20: 150 MB/s P30: 200 MB/s P40-P50: 250 MB/s P60: 480 MB/s P70-P80: 750 MB/s	E10-E50: Up to 60 MB/s E60: Up to 300 MB/s * E70-E80: 500 MB/s *	S4-S50: Up to 60 MB/s S60: Up to 300 MB/s * S70-S80: Up to 500 MB/s *

| Max IOPS per disk | P4: 120 IOPS
P6: 240 IOPS
P10: 500 IOPS
P15: 1100 IOPS
P20: 2300 IOPS
P30: 5000 IOPS
P40-P50: 7500 IOPS
P60: 12,500 IOPS *
P70: 15,000 IOPS *
P80: 20,000 IOPS * | E10-E50: Up to 500 IOPS
E60: Up to 1300 IOPS *
E70-E80: Up to 2000 IOPS * | S4-S50: Up to 500 IOPS
S60: Up to 1300 IOPS *
S70-S80: Up to 2000 IOPS * |

You can find the preceding table at `https://docs.microsoft.com/en-us/azure/storage/storage-about-disks-and-vhds-windows#types-of-disks`.

 At the time of writing this book, there was a new type of disk for Azure Managed Disks, called Ultra SSD; it is most suitable for data-intensive workloads, and provides a disk size of up to 64 TB, with a performance that can be scaled up to 160,000 IOPS and 2 GB/s per disk, with zero downtime.

Adding a data disk to an Azure VM

Nothing is better than getting your hands on some practical implementation after learning about a topic; so, without further ado, let's get started:

1. Navigate to the VM that we created earlier.
2. Navigate to **Disks**, which is under **Settings**, as shown in the following screenshot:

3. You will notice that only the OS disk is added; you may wonder where the temporary disk is. The answer is, it is not here, because as I mentioned earlier, it is a part of the VM physical host. In order to see it, you must open the VM and navigate to **This PC**, as shown in the following screenshot:

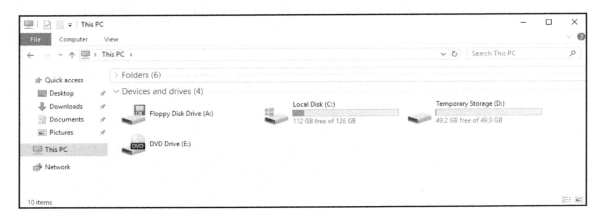

4. Let's go back to our main goal, which is adding a data disk. You have to click on **Add data disk**, and, when you click on **Name**, you will be prompted to select an existing data disk or create a new one. To create a new one, click on **Create disk**:

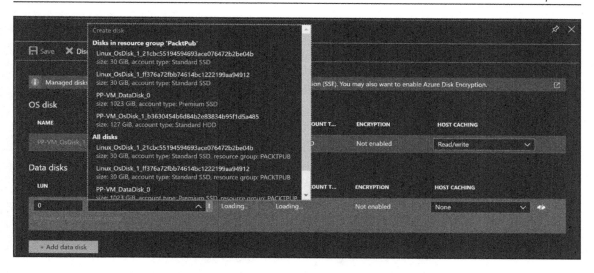

5. Once you have clicked on **Create disk**, a new blade will be opened, where you will have to specify the following:

- **Name**: The disk name.
- **Resource group**: The resource group within which the disk will exist as a resource.
- **Availability zone**: You can (optionally) specify an Availability Zone to deploy the managed disk to (if you have any Availability Zones).
- **Account type**: The type of the disks we have covered earlier.
- **Source type**: You can create the disk from an existing snapshot or a storage blob, or you can create a new one.

- **Size**: This specifies the size of the disk:

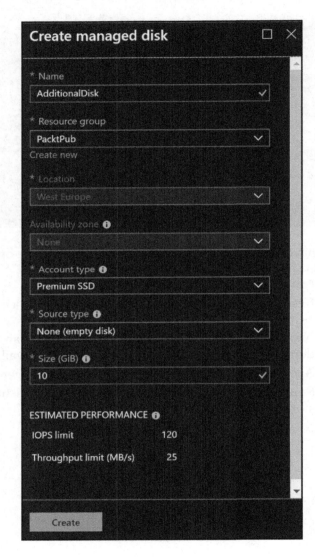

6. When you click on **Create**, you will be navigated back to the **Disks** blade. Save what you have done, as shown in the following screenshot:

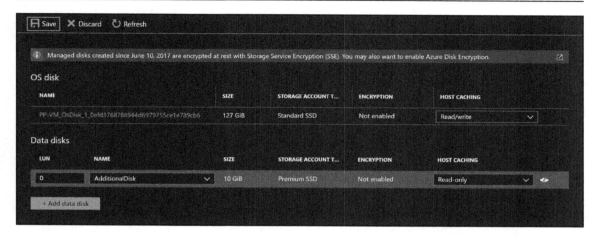

7. When you are done adding the data disk, you will have to open **Disk Management** in the VM; you will be asked to initialize the disk, as shown in the following screenshot:

8. After that, you can do whatever you want to do with the disk, either dividing it into partitions or adding it for future use.

For further information about attaching disks to Linux VMs in Azure, check `https://docs.microsoft.com/en-us/azure/virtual-machines/linux/tutorial-manage-disks#create-and-attach-disks`.

Data disk-key points

The following are some key points to be remembered about data disks:

- Adding more data disks increases the IOPS and throughput, especially if you are using stripping
- Do not use **Full format**, because that will fill the disk clusters with zeros, which means that the disk will appear to be filled with data; as a result, you will have to pay for the whole disk, whether you use it partially or completely
- Trimming is supported from Windows Server 2012/Windows 8, for Windows-based VMs

Expanding disks

If you are using a standard HDD disk, I'd recommend choosing the maximum space allowed for the disk when you create it, because you will only pay for what you use in the storage. For the SSD-based disks, you will pay for the created storage, regardless of its usage. Therefore, if you want to resize the disk size, perform the following steps:

1. Navigate to the VM and stop it; wait until its status changes to **Stopped (deallocated)**.
2. Navigate to **Disks**, which is located under **Settings**.
3. Navigate to the disk that you want to resize.
4. Enter the size that you want the disk to be, as shown in the following screenshot:

5. Then, click on **Save**.

Size reduction is not supported. You can only expand the disk's size. It is a pretty straightforward process, but the main drawback is the downtime that must occur in order to resize the disk.

Host caching

You probably noticed the **Host caching** option while adding and resizing the Azure VM disks, and that is what I am going to cover in this section.

As you know, the VM and its storage do not exist in the same host; so, there is some latency when a VM tries to access its storage, which is represented in OS disks and data disks. Therefore, in order to reduce the latency, Microsoft came up with host caching, which caches the access to the OS and data disks.

There are three types of host caching, as follows:

- **Read-only**: In the read-only host caching mode, the storage will be cached in the VM memory, and, if you use premium storage, it will be cached in the local SSDs; that leads to a very low latency and higher IOPS and throughput for read operations.

- **Read/write**: In the read/write host caching mode, the storage will be cached in the VM memory, and, if you use premium storage, it will be cached in the local SSDs, for all read and write operations; that leads to a better performance for the VM. This mode is the default for the OS disk.
- **None**: In this host caching mode, there will be no data caching; so, whenever an application wants to read or write data, it will have to go all the way to the storage to retrieve it.

Host caching-key points

The following are some key points to be remembered about host caching:

- Use the **None** caching mode for disks on which logs are stored, because logs will do intensive write operations; also, there will be no benefit to using the read-only mode for logs. Therefore, **None** is the best fit in such a situation.
- Use the **read-only** caching mode for disks on which the SQL data that needs to be queried many times from the SQL database, because that will help to lower the latency, and with the data retrieval.
- Do not use **read/write** for just any applications, because the data is cached in the VM memory, and whenever a crash happens in the VM, the data will be lost. So, you have to read more about the application that you are hosting in your VM, in order to know which type of host caching will be the best fit for it. For example, SQL Server has the ability to handle writing cached data to the persistent storage disks, without any intervention.
- Changing the cache settings of an Azure disk detaches and reattaches the target disk. Therefore, consider stopping all applications and services that might be affected before changing this setting.

Azure VM networking

There are many networking configurations that can be set for the VM. You can add additional NICs, change the private IP address, set a private or public IP address to be either static or dynamic, and change the inbound and outbound security rules.

Adding inbound and outbound rules

Adding inbound and outbound security rules to the VM NIC is a very simple process; all you need to do is follow these steps:

1. Navigate to the VM that you want to add inbound/outbound rules to.
2. Scroll down to **Networking**, under **Settings**, as shown in the following screenshot:

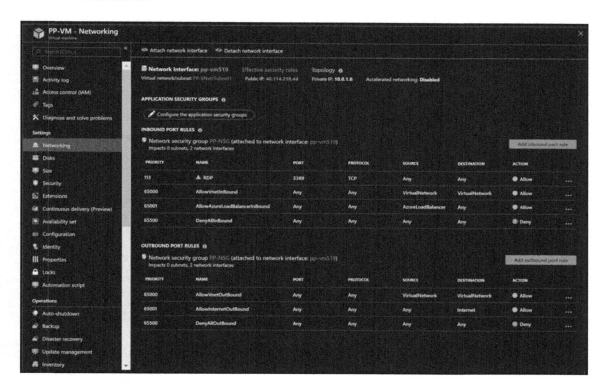

3. To add inbound/outbound rules, click on **Add inbound port rule** or **Add outbound port rule** and follow the steps discussed in the *NSG* section of the previous chapter.

Adding an additional network interface card to the VM

Adding an additional **network interface card (NIC)** starts from the same blade as adding inbound and outbound rules. To add an additional NIC, you perform the following steps:

1. Before adding an additional NIC to the VM, you have to make sure that the VM is in a **Stopped (deallocated)** status.
2. Navigate to **Networking** in the VM that you want to add an NIC to.
3. Click on **Attach network interface**, and a new blade will pop up. Here, you will have to either create a network interface or select an existing one. If you are selecting an existing interface, simply click on **OK**, and you will be done. If you are creating a new interface, click on **Create network interface**, as shown in the following screenshot:

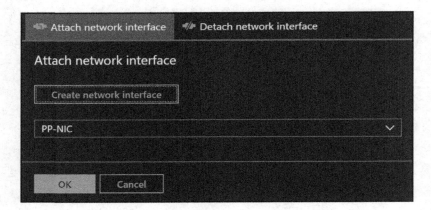

4. A new blade will pop up, where you will have to specify the following:
   - **Name**: The name of the new NIC.
   - **Virtual network**: This field will be grayed out, because you cannot attach a VM's NIC to a different virtual network than the one(s) already attached to it.
   - **Subnet**: Select the desired subnet within the virtual network.
   - **Private IP address assignment**: Specify whether you want to allocate this IP dynamically or statically.
   - **Network security group**: Specify an NSG to be assigned to this NIC.

- **Private IP address (IPv6)**: If you want to assign an IPv6 to this NIC, check this setting.
- **Subscription**: This field will be grayed out, because you cannot have a VM's NICs in a different subscription.
- **Resource group**: Specify the resource group in which the NIC will exist.
- **Location**: This field will be grayed out, because you cannot have VM NICs in different locations:

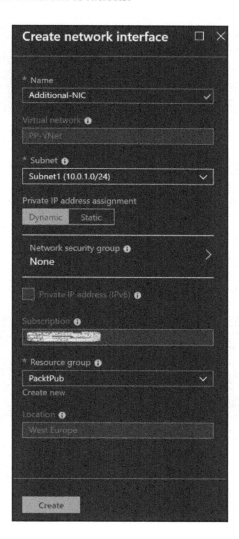

5. Once you have clicked on **Create**, you will return to the previous blade. Here, you will need to specify the NIC that you just created and click on **OK**, as shown in the following screenshot:

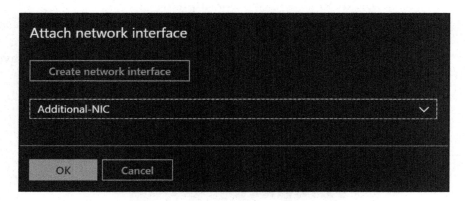

Configuring the NICs

The NICs include some configurations that you might be interested in, as follows:

1. Navigate to the **Network interfaces**.
2. Select the NIC that you want to configure.
3. You can also navigate back to the VM via **Networking**, and then click on the desired NIC, as shown in the following screenshot:

4. To configure the NIC, you need to perform the following steps:

1. Once the NIC blade is open, navigate to **IP configurations**, as shown in the following screenshot:

2. To enable **IP forwarding**, click on **Enabled**, and then click on **Save**. Enabling this feature will cause the NIC to receive traffic that is not destined to its own IP address. Traffic will be sent with a different source IP.

3. To add another IP to the NIC, click on **Add**, and a new blade will pop up, in which you will have to specify the following:

   - **Name**: The name of the IP.
   - **Type**: This field will be grayed out, because a primary IP already exists. Therefore, this one will be secondary.
   - **Allocation**: Specify whether the allocation method is static or dynamic.
   - **IP address**: Enter the static IP address that belongs to the same subnet that the NIC belongs to. If you have selected dynamic allocation, you cannot enter the IP address statically.

- **Public IP address**: Specify whether you need a public IP address for this IP configuration. If you do, you will be asked to configure the required settings:

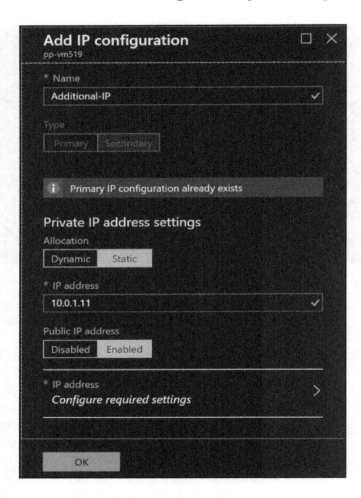

4. Click on **Configure required settings** for the public IP address, and a new blade will pop up, in which you can select an existing public IP address or create a new one, as shown in the following screenshot:

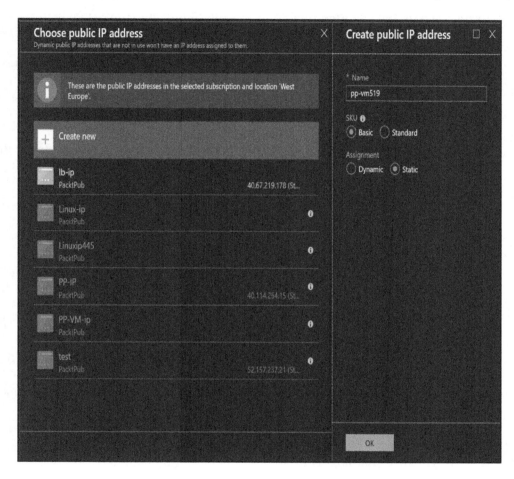

5. When you are done, click on **OK**.

5. If the VM is running, it will be restarted, in order to utilize the new private IP address.

Azure VNet considerations for Azure VMs

Building VMs in Azure is a common task, but to do this task well (and to make the VMs operate properly), you have to understand the considerations for Azure VNets in Azure VMs. These considerations are as follows:

- Azure VNets enable you to bring your own IPv4/IPv6 addresses and assign them to Azure VMs, statically or dynamically.
- You do not have access to the role that acts as DHCP or provides IP addresses; you can only control the ranges that you want to use in the form of address ranges and subnets.
- Installing a DHCP role on one of the Azure VMs is currently unsupported; this is because Azure does not use traditional layer-2 or layer-3 topology, and instead uses layer-3 traffic with tunneling, to emulate a layer-2 LAN.
- Private IP addresses can be used for internal communication; external communication can be done via public IP addresses.
- You can assign multiple private and public IP addresses to a single VM.
- You can assign multiple NICs to a single VM.
- By default, all of the VMs within the same virtual network can communicate with each other, unless otherwise specified by an NSG on a subnet within the virtual network.
- The NSG can sometimes cause overhead; without this overhead, however, all VMs within the same subnet would communicate with each other.
- The inbound security rules are first applied on the NSG of the subnet, and then the VM NIC NSG; for example, if the subnet's NSG allows HTTP traffic, it will pass through it. However, it may not reach its destination if the VM NIC NSG does not allow it.
- The outbound security rules are applied for the VM NIC NSG first, and then applied on the subnet NSG.
- Multiple NICs assigned to a VM can exist in different subnets.
- Azure VMs with multiple NICs in the same availability set do not have to have the same number of NICs, but the VMs must have at least two NICs.
- When you attach an NIC to a VM, you need to ensure that they exist in the same location and subscription.
- The NIC and the VNet must exist in the same subscription and location.
- The NIC's MAC address cannot be changed until the VM to which the NIC is assigned is deleted.

- Once the VM is created, you cannot change the VNet to which it is assigned; however, you can change the subnet to which the VM is assigned.
- You cannot attach an existing NIC to a VM during its creation, but you can add an existing NIC as an additional NIC.
- In a multi-NIC VM, the NSG that is applied to one NIC does not affect the others.

Summary

In this chapter, we covered some of the most interesting elements of Azure VMs, as well as how to configure them and properly design a VM's storage and networking.

In the next chapter, we'll introduce one of the most commonly used Azure PaaS solutions: Azure Web Apps.

Questions

1. What state would the VM turn into if you shut it down from inside the OS?
   - Stopped
   - Shutdown
   - Stopped (deallocated)

2. Which VM series is the oldest of the following options?
   - B-Series
   - A-Series
   - D-Series

3. What is the recommended disk to store paging files?
   - OS disk
   - Temporary disk
   - Data disk

4. Which statement is true about Availability Sets?
   - VMs must have the same number of NICs
   - Each VM can only have one NIC
   - VMs in the same availability set should have at least two NICs

Further reading

- IP Forwarding (https://docs.microsoft.com/en-us/azure/virtual-network/virtual-network-network-interface#enable-or-disable-ip-forwarding)
- VM scale set (https://docs.microsoft.com/en-us/azure/virtual-machine-scale-sets/overview)
- Availability Zones (https://docs.microsoft.com/en-us/azure/availability-zones/az-overview)
- VM images (https://docs.microsoft.com/en-us/azure/virtual-machines/windows/capture-image-resource)

Azure Web Apps Basics 5

In this chapter, we will be introducing Azure App Service, App Service Environment and its types. We will then cover App Service plans and the different pricing plans on offer in order to understand which plan will fulfill your needs. Lastly, you will learn how to create these service in the Azure portal.

The following topics will be covered in this chapter:

- Introduction to Azure App Service
- App Service plans
- App Service Environment
- Creating an App Service plan
- Creating an App Service

Introduction to Azure App Service

Azure App Service is one of Microsoft Azure's **Platform as a service (PaaS)** offerings. It is used to run your applications on Azure in a fully managed service environment.

This offering provides the following services:

- **Web Apps**: Used to host your web apps that need to scale with your business
- **API Apps**: Used to easily build and consume APIs on the cloud
- **Mobile Apps**: Used to build mobile apps for any device
- **Logic apps**: Used to automate business processes across **Software as a service (SaaS)** and on-premises systems
- **Function apps**: Used to integrate systems, work with IoT, process data, and even build simple APIs and microservices.

In this chapter, we will be focusing on Azure Web Apps specifically.

Azure Web Apps

As mentioned earlier, Azure Web Apps is one of the Azure App Service. Azure Web Apps runs on top of **virtual machines (VMs)**, where a lot of IIS clusters are deployed in Microsoft data centers. Therefore, when you want to deploy your own web app, you do not have to be responsible for deploying and managing the VMs—just build your app and deploy it on Azure Web Apps.

You can deploy web apps built using one of the following languages: .NET, .NET Core, PHP, Ruby, Python, Java, and Node.js. These apps can be hosted on Windows, Linux, or even in containers such as Docker, although this mode is still in preview at the time of writing.

App Service plans

When you create an App Service, such as a Web App for example, you will be asked to specify the App Service plan.

An App Service plan is like the hardware host on which you run your VMs. It contains the resources that are shared among the App Service. As a result, we can look at App Service as VMs running on the host, which is the App Service plan.

The App Service plan also defines many settings for the App Service that will be built on it, such as the region, number of instances, whether it will be able to scale out/in or not, and much more, which will be covered later on.

Azure offers different plans to fulfill different customers' needs, such as the following:

- **Shared infrastructure plans**:
    - **Free plan**: This is the entry level plan, and as its name implies, it's available for free. It's meant for dev/test scenarios, or if you wish to deploy a website for temporary purposes, where your app would be running with other apps on the same VM with a limited CPU quota per day and no SLA guarantee. This option is suitable, as long as you don't care about your domain name.
    - **Shared plan**: This plan is also meant for dev/test scenarios, but offers a higher CPU quota than the free plan, and the ability to add a custom domain name to the app. This is the lowest cost plan.

- **Dedicated infrastructure plans**:
    - **Basic plan**: Although this plan is meant for dev/test scenarios, it can also be considered as the entry level for a small business. Also, it provides a dedicated VM with an OS (Windows/Linux) of your choice on which the apps will be run, greater hardware resources for your apps, the ability to add SSL certificates to secure your apps, and manual scaling up to three instances. Unlike the shared plans, it offers a 99.95% SLA.
    - **Standard plan**: This plan offers more resources than the previous plans. It also offers autoscaling, deployment slots, distribution of traffic using Traffic Manager, and daily backups.
    - **Premium plan**: This plan offers even more advanced hardware resources, more deployment slots than the standard plans, and more instances when it comes to scalability. There's the Premium plan and Premium V2 plan. The advantage of the Premium V2 plan is that it runs on a Dv2 series VM.
    - **Isolated infrastructure plan**: This plan offers an isolated hosting environment that is located in its own virtual networks and virtual machines. Like the Premium V2 plan, it is based on the Dv2 virtual machine series. It offers the other features available with similar level plans, but with higher specifications.

 Deployment slots provide the ability to develop and test your app without affecting the production environment. Whenever you want to swap the dev/test environment with the production one, you can do it with one click, without causing any downtime. Also, if you find something wrong with the new release of your application, you can roll back by swapping to the slot that used to run the production before.

Azure App Service Environments

Generally speaking, when you deploy an App Service on an App Service plan, these apps will be deployed in a multi-tenant environment. In other words, the VMs that will host the apps will be in a shared pool, hosting other customers' apps as well.

Azure's App Service Environment will not do this. Instead, it will provide you with an isolated environment, such as that available on the isolated service plan, which needs an App Service Environment to function in a way that takes advantage of the benefits it offers.

App Service Environment provides the following benefits:

- Isolation—you will run your own app on a single tenant, so you can make it compliant with your policy standards
- Bring your own virtual network—you can use specific virtual networks for the VMs running your App Service, giving you more control over the traffic flow
- Support for scaling app instances can reach up to 100 instances at the time of writing

App Service Environment types

App Service Environment is available in a number of different types and versions.

Azure's App Service Environment has the following versions:

- **App Service Environment v1**: This version has the common benefits of App Service Environments, discussed previously
- **App Service Environment v2**: This version comes with fewer complications, as you will not have to configure frontends and workers to auto-scale your App Service plan.

Azure App Service Environment offerings are also divided along the lines of accessibility:

- **External**: This type exposes the apps on App Service Environment to allow for access via the internet by either the public IP address assigned to it, or the external domain name provided by Azure, such as `*.p.azurewebsites.net` or a custom domain name.
- **Internal**: This type exposes the apps internally on the virtual network it is built on, via an internal load balancer. If you want to expose it to the internet, you will have to add a custom domain name that will resolve to the internal load balancer, as it does not provide any external domain names, nor a public IP address.

Creating an App Service Environment

Creating an App Service Environment is not a hard process. To do it, perform the following steps:

1. Navigate to Azure portal, and search for `app service environments`, as shown in the following screenshot:

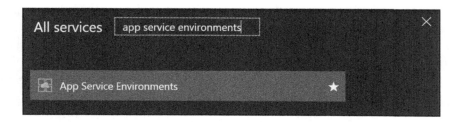

2. Click on it, and a new blade will be opened where you can view or add new App Service Environments, as shown in the following screenshot:

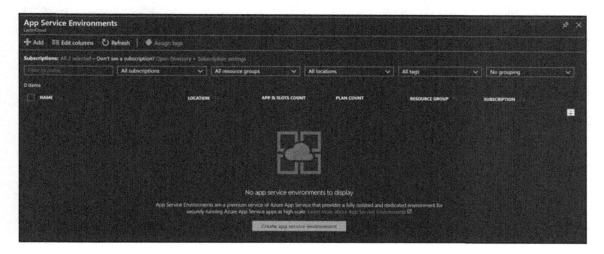

3. To add a new App Service Environment, click on **Add** and a new blade will be opened, where you have to specify the following:

- **Name**: Specify the name for the app service environment
- **Subscription**: Select the subscription that will be charged for using this service
- **Resource group**: Specify the resource group within which the app service environment will exist as a resource.
- **Virtual Network/Location**: When you click on it, a new blade will be opened where you have to specify the following:
  - **Virtual Network**: Either create a new one or select an existing one
  - **VIP type**: This is the accessibility type that we covered earlier; choose external or internal:

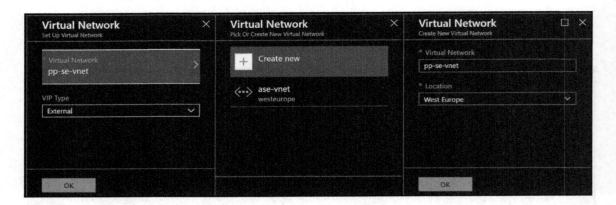

- Once you specify the previous settings, you will be asked to specify the subnet in the virtual network where the App Service Environment will exist:

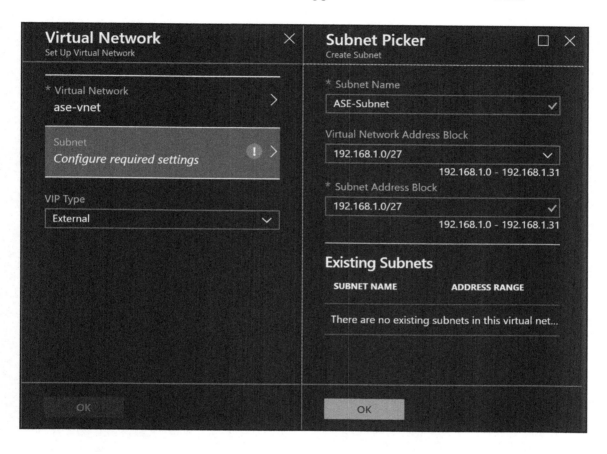

- **App Service Environment pricing details**: If you want more information about the pricing, you can click on the pricing details option, which will open a new blade displaying the App Service Environment pricing details:

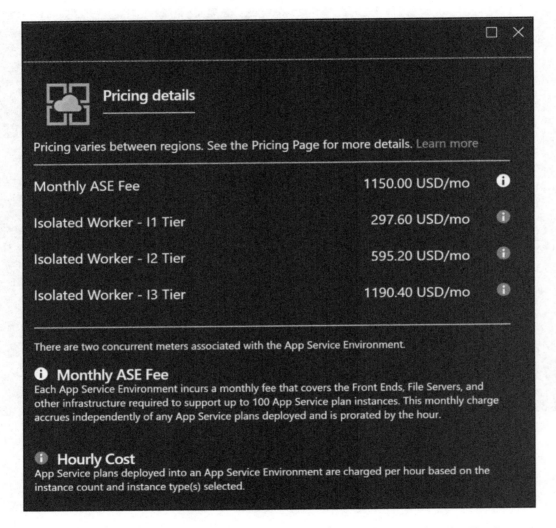

4. Once you are done with specifying the settings of the App Service Environment, you can click on **Create** to start creating App Service Environment.

- It will take a while for your App Service Environment to be created.
- The location of the virtual network you assign to the App Service Environment is the region within which the App Service Environment will operate.
- If you are going to use an existing virtual network for your App Service Environment, make sure that it has spare IPs to create a dedicated subnet for the App Service Environment. Providing an external App Service Environment with no service plans will use 12 IP addresses of the subnet, and the internal one with the same specifications will use 13 IP addresses.
- You can only have one App Service Environment per subscription.
- App Service Environment can only be used with Isolated App Service plan.
- We will be using App Service Environment for demo purposes. Delete App Service Environment once you are done with the demo, because it is a very expensive service.

Creating an App Service plan

With the information we have seen so far, you should be excited to get started and create an App Service plan. Therefore, without further ado, let's get started:

1. Navigate to the Azure portal and search for `app service plans`, as shown in the following screenshot:

2. A new blade will be opened, where you can view/add new App Service plans, as shown in the following screenshot:

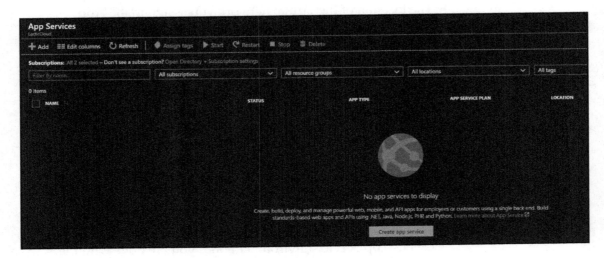

3. When you click on **Add**, a new blade will be opened where you have to specify the following:
   - **App Service plan**: Specify a descriptive name for the plan
   - **Subscription**: Specify the subscription that will be charged for using this service
   - **Resource group**: Specify the resource group in which the app service plan will exist as a resource.
   - **Operating system**: Specify whether the plan is Windows-based or Linux-based
   - **Location**: Select the region where you want to deploy your app service plan

- **Pricing tier**: Specify the App Service plan that suits your needs, as shown in the following screenshot:

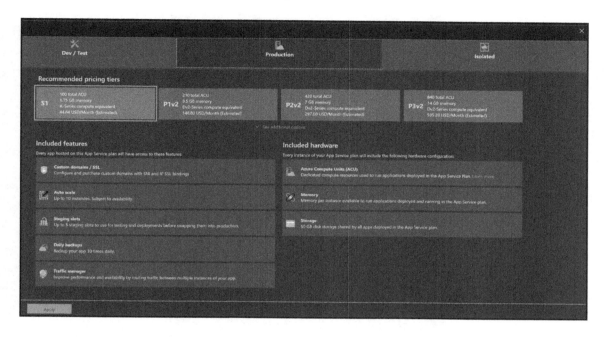

4. Once you are done with specifying the required settings, you can start the creation of the App Service plan by clicking on **Create**:

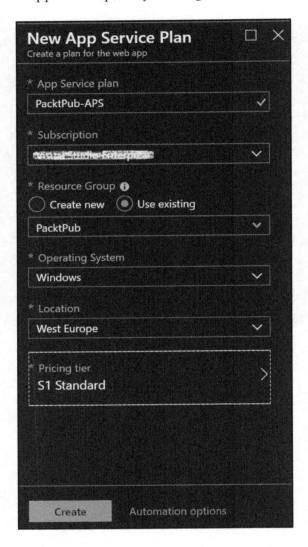

If you want to build the App Service plan within the App Service Environment, you need to select the App Service Environment as the location for the App Service plan.

Creating an App Service

Creating an App Service is a very straightforward process too. To do it, perform the following steps:

1. Navigate to the Azure portal and search for `App Services`:

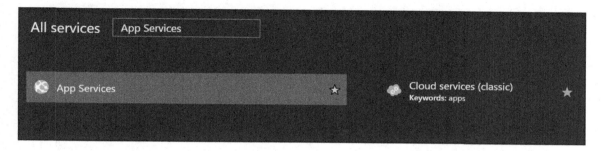

2. When you click on it, a new blade will be opened, where you can view/add App Service:

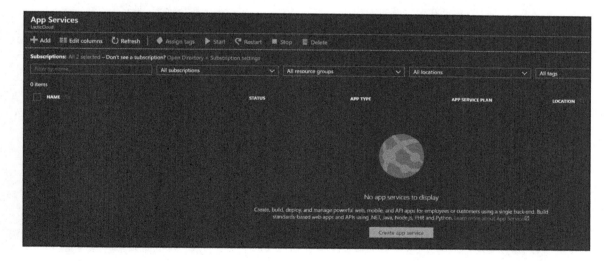

3. When you click on **Add**, a new blade will be opened, where you can select from different App Service and even some templates for HTML5, WordPress, Joomla, and much more:

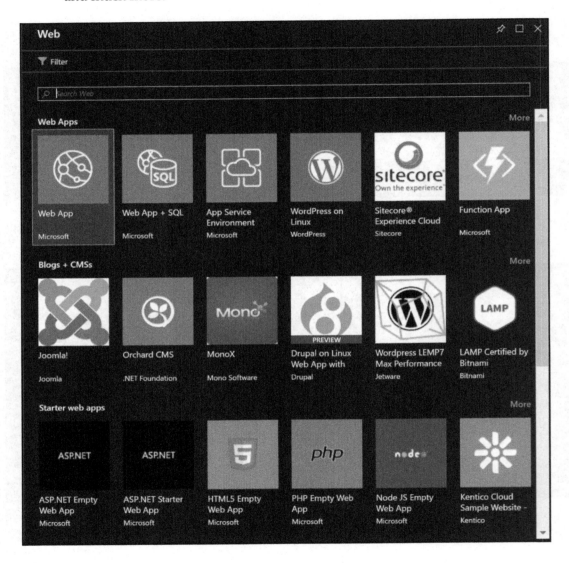

4. In our case, we will select **Web App**. Once selected, you will be navigated to a new blade, which will give you an overview of Azure Web Apps:

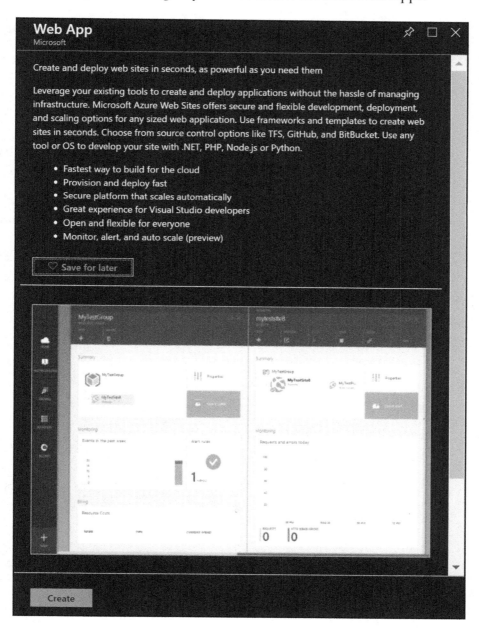

5. Next, click on **Create**, which will open a new blade where you have to specify the following:

- **App name**: Specify a name for your app
- **Subscription**: Select the subscription that will be charged for using this service
- **Resource Group**: Specify the resource group in which the app will exist as a resource
- **OS**: Linux or Windows
- **Publish**: Specify whether you want to publish code directly to the App Service, or to a container within which a Docker image will be running. If you select a container, you will be asked to configure it.
- **App Service plan/Location**: Select an existing App Service plan or create a new one.
- **Application Insights**: This solution will help you to detect and diagnose quality issues in your web apps and web services, and help you understand what your users are actually doing with them. At the time of writing, you can turn it on for Windows-based web apps that are not published via Docker images

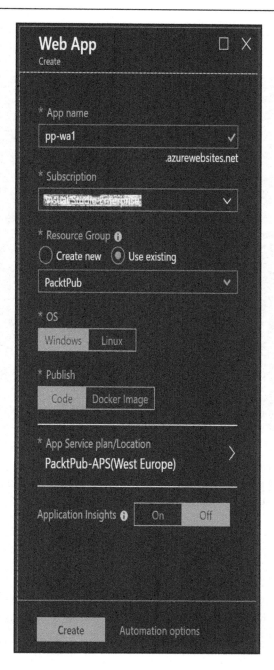

6. Once you are done, click on **Create**.

7. Once the app is created, you can navigate to it, and in the **Overview** blade, you will note that you can **Browse**, **Stop**, **Restart**, and much more:

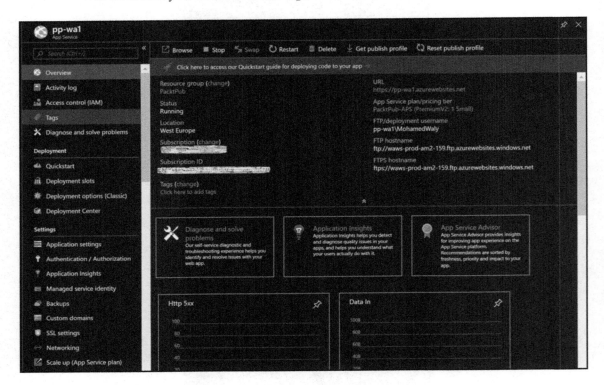

You cannot select an OS for a web app different than the App Service plan. The App Service must operate in the same region as that of the App Service plan.

Summary

In this chapter on Azure App Service, we were introduced to some highlights of App Service plans and App Service Environments, so you can now specify the differences between them, and how and when to use each one.

In the next chapter, you will learn more about Azure Web Apps and how to manage them in a way that will provide a highly reliable solution.

Questions

1. Which of the following apps are supported by Azure App Service?
   - Web apps and desktop apps
   - Function apps and logic apps
   - None of them

2. Which of the following App Service plans support adding custom domain names?
   - Shared
   - Basic
   - Standard
   - All of them

3. You can run a Linux App service on a Windows App Service plan?
   - True
   - False

Further reading

- *Use an App Service Environment* (https://docs.microsoft.com/en-us/azure/app-service/environment/using-an-ase)
- *App Service plans* (https://azure.microsoft.com/en-us/pricing/details/app-service/plans/)

Managing Azure Web Apps

6

In this chapter, we will continue discussing Azure Web Apps and how to work with them. The chapter will be kicked off by looking at deployment slots, which help you to have multiple environments for testing and development, while not affecting the production environment. Then, the application settings of the App Service in Azure will be covered. This is followed by a discussion of the scalability solutions offered for App Service. Finally, we will go through the backup process of the App Service.

The following topics will be covered in this chapter:

- Deployment slots
- App Service application settings
- Azure App Service scalability
- Azure App Service backup

Deployment slots

Deployment slots is one of Azure App Service greatest features. With deployment slots in place, you shouldn't be worried if your new release doesn't work appropriately when it is released to production. This is because you can have different slots for dev/test purposes and a different slot for production.

Using deployment slots, you can verify that the application is functioning properly before publishing it. Then, you can swap it with the production slot, which will cause almost no downtime. If the application does not behave as expected, you can swap it with the application that was working in production right before you swapped the slots. When you create an App Service, it's running on the default production slot.

To add an additional deployment slot, follow these steps:

1. Navigate to the App Service that you want to add another deployment slot to.
2. Under **Deployment**, click on **Deployment slots**, as shown in the following screenshot:

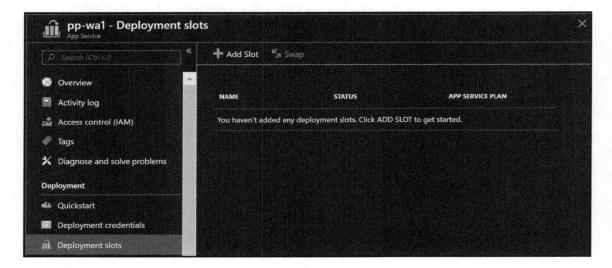

3. Click on **Add Slot**, and a new blade will pop up where you have to specify the following:
   - **Name**: Specify a descriptive name for the slot.
   - **Configuration Source**: Specify whether you want to clone the configuration from another slot or not:

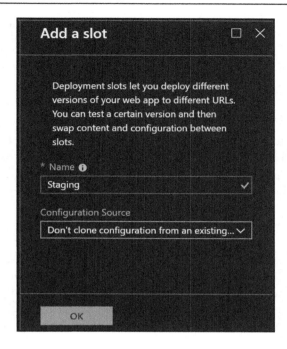

Deployment slots key points

The following key points will give you more information about deployment slots:

- If you have cloned the configuration of one of the deployment slots, you can edit these configurations later.
- When you swap a deployment slot with another, you will note that some of the settings will be swapped, while others won't:
    - The following are the settings that will be swapped:
        - Handler mappings
        - WebJobs content
        - App settings (unless they are stuck to a slot)
        - General settings, such as web sockets, framework version, and 32/64 bit
        - Connection strings (unless they are stuck to a slot)
        - Monitoring and diagnostic settings

- The following are settings that won't be swapped:
    - Custom domain names
    - Scale settings
    - SSL certificates and bindings
    - Publishing endpoints
    - WebJobs scheduler
- Before swapping, make sure that the settings that haven't been swapped are properly configured in the staging slot to avoid any failures after swapping.
- When you swap slots, the traffic will be redirected to the swapped slot and no requests will be dropped. Therefore, you will notice no downtime.

App Service application settings

Each App Service you will create in Azure will have some app settings to configure. These app settings are some configurable items that you would like to configure for the app without changing any piece of the code. The application settings of the App Service can be accessed by navigating to App Service and select the App Service you wish and click on **Application settings**.

The application settings are classified into the following categories:

- **General settings**: Here, you can specify the following:
    - **Framework**: Framework versions that the app is using, such as .NET, PHP, Java, and Python.
    - **Platform**: Specify the platform architecture that you want to run your web app on, whether it is 32 bit or 64 bit.
    - **Web sockets**: You can enable web sockets for your applications in case your web app is using socket.io or ASP.NET SignalR. In addition to that, web sockets allow for more flexible connectivity between web apps and modern browsers. Your web app would need to be built to leverage these capabilities.

- **Always On**: This setting would load your web app all the time, because by default, web apps are unloaded after they have been idle for a while. It's recommended to enable this setting if you have continuous WebJobs running on the web app.
- **Managed pipeline version**: This setting identifies the IIS application pool mode. It's recommended to use the integrated mode unless you have a legacy application that depends on IIS versions older than IIS 7; then you can select **Classic**.
- **HTTP version**: Select the HTTP version that suits your needs.
- **ARR affinity**: If you turn on this setting, it will ensure that the client is routed to the same VM when you have multiple VMs hosting your web app during the life of the session.
- **Auto swap**: This setting can be configured for any deployment slot, other than the production one. In order to configure it for a deployment slot, you have to navigate to App Service then select **Deployment slots** and then select the deployment slot you want to configure this setting for. A new blade will be opened for the deployment slots with the same configurations in the blade of the original App Service, from there you can click on **Application settings** to be able to view the app settings of the slot and configure it accordingly. Therefore, if this setting is enabled, it will automatically swap this slot with the slot that you will specify in the next step whenever an update is pushed to that slot.
- **Auto swap slot**: If the previous setting is enabled, you have to specify which slot you should swap.

- **FTP access**: Specify the way in which FTP accesses the App Service, whether by enabling it for FTP and FTPS, or FTPS only, or just disable it if you do not want to use it:

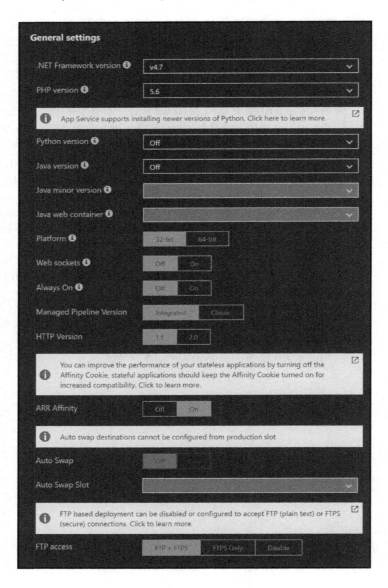

- **Debugging**: In this category, you can specify the following:
  - **Remote debugging**: You can specify whether you want to enable or disable remote debugging for this App Service. If it is enabled, the remote debugger of Visual Studio can be connected directly to the web app.
  - **Remote Visual Studio version**: Specify the version of Visual Studio you have. Only the **2015** and **2017** versions are supported at the time of writing:

- **Application settings:** In this category, you can provide some settings that you want to force your web application to load on every startup in the form of name/value pairs. For example, if you want to configure the application to be monitored by Application Insights, you can set the application setting's name and value, as shown in the following screenshot:

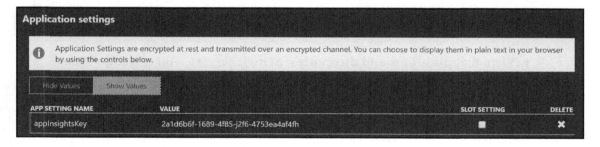

 If you want to stick this setting to this slot only, you have to tick on **SLOT SETTING**.

- **Connection strings**: You can specify the connection strings between the application and the databases.
- **Default documents**: In this category, you can specify the documents that would be displayed at the home page of the web app.

- **Handler mappings**: In this category, you can add custom script processors so you can handle requests based on a specific file extension by specifying the following:
  - **Extension**: The extension of the file you want to be handled.
  - **Script processor path**: This is an absolute path to the script processor that will operate to process requests for files that corresponds to the pattern specified in the extension.
  - **Optional arguments**: This can be used to add another path to a script for the script processor. Therefore, any arguments you would like to specify when the script processor is enabled can be proceeded with.

 The script processor is responsible for executing the scripts that would be stored in the **SCRIPT PROCESSOR** path.

- **Virtual applications and directories**: In this category, you can add virtual applications and directories, where you can specify the virtual directory and its physical path according to the root of the website.

 For more information about the application settings, check the following article: https://docs.microsoft.com/en-us/azure/app-service/web-sites-configure.

Application settings key points

The following key points will give you more information about application settings:

- If you want to specify a 64-bit environment for the web app, you need to make sure that the plan is in the basic tier at the least, because it does not support the free or shared hosting plans.

- If you want to improve the performance of stateless applications, ensure that the **ARR affinity** setting is disabled, because stateless applications don't save the client data generated in a session to be used in the next one, and that might lead to some instances serving more requests than other servers. However, if it is disabled, the load balancer will be able to distribute the traffic evenly.
- If you have Traffic Manager in place to load balance the traffic, it is recommended to disable **ARR affinity**, because Traffic Manager does not support sticky sessions.
- The key/value pairs you will be providing as application settings will be encrypted when stored.
- The connection strings are encrypted when stored.

Azure App Service scalability

In this section, I'll be discussing the scalability options for Azure App Service. Using these scalability solutions will help you to have a highly available application.

There are two types of supported scalability:

- **Scaleup**: Here, you increase the size of the resources on which the web app operates. For example, memory, CPU, and disk space.
- **Scaleout**: Here, you increase the number of instances on which the apps operate. For example, if you are facing a high load over the instance on which the web app operates, another one will be created to load balance with it.

Scaling up

When you notice that your application is consuming too many of the App Service plan's resources, you can scale the App Service plan up. This gives it more resources so that it can fulfill the application's needs.

When you scale up an App Service plan, you get more hardware resources, such as CPU, memory, and storage.

You will also get more supportability for features, such as the following:

- Custom domain/SSL
- The number of instances you can auto scale to
- The number of staging slots you can have

- The number of daily backups of your applications that you can make
- Traffic Manager

To scale up the App Service plan that your application is a part of, follow these steps:

1. Navigate to the Azure portal and then to App Service. Choose the App Service you want to scale up and then select **Scale up (App Service plan)**, as shown in the following screenshot:

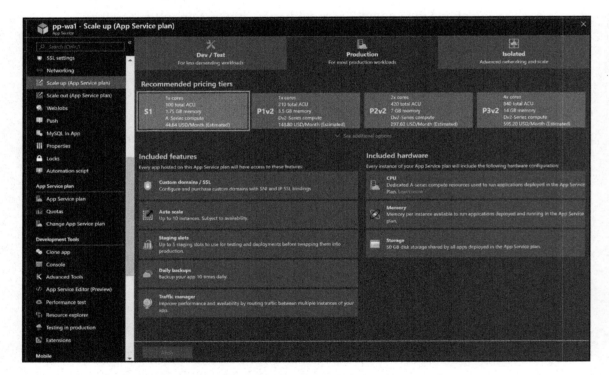

2. Then, select a plan that fits your criteria and click on **Apply**.
3. You can also scale up the App Service plan if you know which plan your application is a part of by navigating to **App Service plans**. From here, select the App Service plan you want to scale up and click **Scale up (App service Plan)**, as shown in the following screenshot:

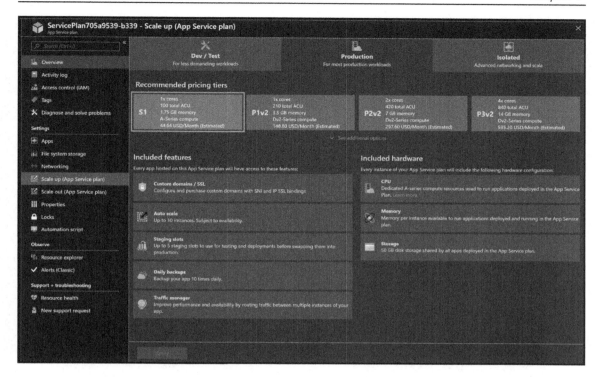

4. Once you are done, click on **Apply**.

App Service plan scaleup key points

The following key points will give you more information about the App Service plan:

- When you scale up an App Service plan, it affects all of the applications within this plan in a matter of seconds, provided that you do not have to either change anything in the code or redeploy the application.
- When you notice that the use of your apps is decreasing, you can scale it down. Otherwise, you will be still charged for the pricing tier you have scaled up to because it has reserved a VM that's running in the background.

Scaling out

Scaling out is a credible solution for applications that have usage peaks from time to time. By scaling out, you can increase the number of instances (VMs) in which the App Service are running instead of increasing the hardware resources of it. You can also enable auto scale. By doing this, when a specific threshold is triggered, the App Service plan will be scaled out to handle the load.

There are two ways to scale out your App Service plan, and we will discuss these options in the upcoming sections.

Scaling out the App Service plan manually

To scale out the App Service plan manually, you need to follow these steps:

1. Navigate to App Service. Choose the App Service you want to scale up and then click **Scale out (App Service plan)**, as shown in the following screenshot:

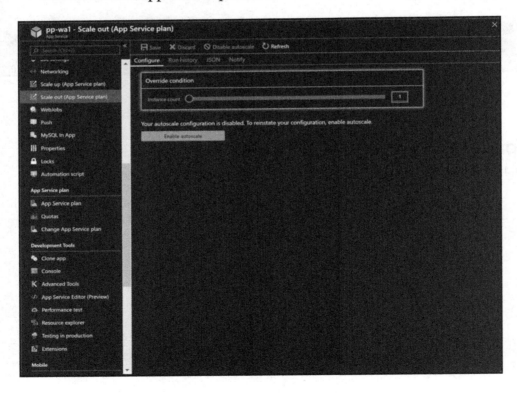

2. Then, you can increase the number of instances up to the number you want to scale out to.

3. Once you are done, click on **Save**.

You can also do the same by navigating to **App Service plans**, selecting the App Service plan you want to scale out, and then choosing **Scale out (App Service plan)**.

Scaling out the App Service plan automatically

To scale out the App Service plan automatically, you need to follow these steps:

1. Navigate to App Service and choose the App Service you want to scale out.
2. Click on **Enable autoscale**.
3. Then, you will need to configure the autoscale settings by specifying the following:
     - **Autoscale setting name**: Specify a descriptive name for the purpose of the autoscale
     - **Resource group**: Specify a resource group for the autoscale setting
     - **Scale conditions**: You can add scale conditions according to your needs by specifying the following:
          - **Scale mode**:
               - **Scale based on a metric**: Specify a metric based on which a scale out will be performed. For example, when CPU usage exceeds 70%, it will add one more instance.
               - **Scale to a specific instance count**: Specify the number of instances you want to scale to. If you have selected this option, you do not have to proceed with the upcoming settings.

- **Rules**: Click on **Add a rule** to create a rule that will determine how the App Service plan will scale out/in. A new blade will open where you have to specify the following:

  - **Metric source**: Specify the source for which you will specify metrics that will determine the scale out/in.
  - **Resource type**: If you have selected **Other resource** in the metric source, you will have to specify the resource type.
  - **Resource**: If you have selected a metric source other than the current resource, you will need to specify that source. For example, if you selected **Storage queue** as a metric source, you will have to specify which storage account to use as a resource.
  - **Time aggregation**: This is the aggregation method that's used to aggregate sampled metrics. For example, *time aggregation = average* will aggregate the sampled metrics by taking the average of them.
  - **Metric name**: Specify which metric you want to measure so that the rule can determine whether to scale out/in.
  - **Time grain statistic**: This is the aggregation method within the *timeGrain* period. For example, *statistic = average* and *timeGrain = PT1M* means that the metrics will be aggregated every 1 minute by taking the average.

- **Operator**: Specify the measure operator that will specify when the value of the metric has exceeded the threshold. For example, this operator will specify when the actual value of the resource is greater, lesser, equal to, and so on, compared to the threshold.
- **Threshold**: This is the threshold on which the action will be performed to specify whether the plan scales out/in.
- **Duration**: This is the duration of time required to look back for metrics. For example, 10 minutes means that every time autoscale runs, it will query metrics for the past 10 minutes. This allows the metrics to stabilize and avoids reacting to transient spikes.
- **Operation**: Specify whether to decrease or increase instances count/percentage when a threshold is exceeded.
- **Instance count**: The instance count will be increased/decreased according to the operation you specified in the previous step.

- **Cool down**: The amount of time to wait after a scale operation before scaling again. For example, if the cool-down time is 10 minutes and a scale operation has just occurred, autoscale will not attempt to scale again until after 10 minutes. This is to allow the metrics to stabilize first. The following screenshot shows the scale rule:

- **Instance limits**: There are three instance limits that need to be specified
    - **Minimum**: Specifies the minimum instance count.
    - **Maximum**: Specifies the maximum instance count.
    - **Default**: If there's a problem reading the resource metrics and the current capacity is below the default capacity, then to ensure the availability of the resource, autoscale will scale out to the default. If the current capacity is already higher than the default capacity, autoscale will not scale in.
- **Schedule**: By default, the first added rule is executed when none of the other scale conditions match. If you are adding other conditions, you can specify the start/end date or specific days for the rule:

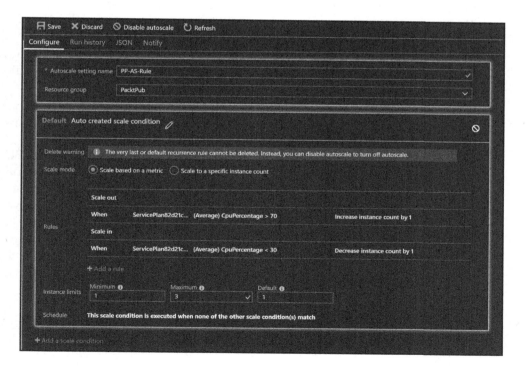

4. Once you are done, click on **Save**.

Key points for autoscaling your App Service plan

The following key points will give you more information about App Service plan autoscaling:

- You cannot assign more than one autoscale setting to one resource.
- When you have more than one instance, the threshold will be calculated according to the average of the metric across all of the instances. This is done to decide whether to scale out/in.
- If you want to investigate an autoscale operation failure, you can use the activity log.
- Make sure that you have different values for the minimum and maximum number of instances with a reasonable margin.
- If you have manually scaled out/in at the same time that you have autoscale rules, the autoscale rules will overwrite the manual scaling you have done.
- Ensure that you have scale out and scale in rules so that you can get benefits from the usage savings. For example, when the App Service plan scales out after hitting a threshold, it can be scaled in again after going below another threshold that indicates that the resource usage is quite acceptable to be scaled in.
- It is not recommended to set the scale out/in rules threshold when it goes above or below the same value. For example, do not make the threshold for the scale out when it is above 70% and scale in when it is below 70%.
- If you have added multiple rules to the same autoscale setting, it will scale out when any scaleout rule is met, but it will not scale in until all of the scale-in rules are met to maintain the performance and the availability of the apps. For example, if we have different scale in rules, such as a scale-in rule for the CPU and another one for the memory, and then one of these rules is met but the other is not. In this case, the scale in will not be triggered to maintain the performance because we have another rule that would affect the performance that not been met yet.
- When the metrics are not available, it will use the default number of instances. Therefore, make sure that you have set a reasonable number of instances so that you can get your apps up and running with no negative impact on performance.

Azure App Service backup

To avoid any unexpected scenarios regarding your apps, it is recommended that you back up your apps regularly. Therefore, in the worst-case scenario, you can retrieve your application with minimal data loss.

To configure backup for your app, follow these steps:

1. Navigate to the App Service you want to back up.
2. Under **Settings**, click on **Backup**, as shown in the following screenshot:

3. When you click on **Configure**, a new blade will open where you have to specify the following:
    - **Storage settings**: Specify a container in a storage account where the backup will be stored. If you do not have a storage account, you will have to create one.
    - **Backup schedule**: Specify whether you want to run the backup based on a schedule or not. If you enabled scheduling, you will have to specify the following:
        - **Backup every**: Specify the frequency of the backup either in days or hours.

- **Specify backup schedule from**: Specify when to trigger the backup schedule for the first time.
- **Retention**: Specify for how long you want to retain the backup files. You can set it to **0** to keep the backup files indefinitely.
- **Keep at least one backup**: Specify whether you want to keep at least one backup or not.

4. If you want to back up the database of the app, tick **INCLUDE IN BACKUP** to back it up too. If you have other backup policies for your databases, you do not have to include it:

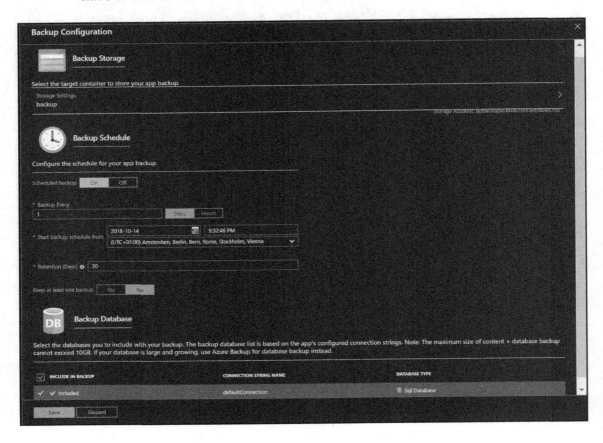

App Service backup key points

The following key points will give you more information about App Service backup:

- Ensure that the storage account in which you are going to store your backup is in the same subscription as the App Service. At the time of writing, it only supports the general-purpose storage account v1 as a storage account type.
- The backup size should not exceed 10 GB of the application and its database (if the database is backed up too). Otherwise, an error will occur.
- You cannot back up an SSL-enabled Azure MySQL database.
- Do not use firewall-enabled storage accounts to store the backup of your apps.
- If you want to back up the database of an application, but you cannot find it displayed under the **Backup Database**, ensure that its connection string has been added in the application settings.

Summary

So far, we have covered the most important parts of Azure Web apps. In this chapter, we continued the journey that was started in the previous chapter by covering some of the interesting solutions, such as the deployment slots, the App Service settings, scalability, and how to back up your App Service.

In the next chapter, I'll start to talk about Azure SQL Databases, which will help you to understand how to work and manage your SQL Databases on Azure.

Questions

1. WebJobs content is swapped between the deployment slots:
   - True
   - False

2. Under which settings can you add a connection to the database?
   - General settings
   - Connection strings
   - Default documents
   - Handler mappings

3. Increasing the number of instances on which is the web app is running refers to:
   * Scaleout
   * Scaleup
4. What is the mandatory requirement for backing up App Service?
   * Database
   * Storage account
   * Azure Site Recovery

Further reading

* *Azure App Service Hybrid Connections* (`https://docs.microsoft.com/en-us/azure/app-service/app-service-hybrid-connections`)
* *Controlling Azure App Service traffic with Azure Traffic Manager* (`https://docs.microsoft.com/en-us/azure/app-service/web-sites-traffic-manager`)
* *How to: Monitor Apps in Azure App Service* (`https://docs.microsoft.com/en-us/azure/app-service/web-sites-monitor`)
* *Run Background tasks with WebJobs in Azure App Service* (`https://docs.microsoft.com/en-us/azure/app-service/web-sites-create-web-jobs`)
* *Publish a Web app to Azure App Service using Visual Studio* (`https://docs.microsoft.com/en-us/visualstudio/deployment/quickstart-deploy-to-azure?view=vs-2017`)

Basics of Azure SQL Database

7

In this chapter, we will go through one of the trendiest topics for IT professionals, developers, and DBAs: Azure SQL Database. This chapter will be kicked off by an introduction to Azure SQL Database. We'll look at why you should use this service and the difference between SQL Database in the IaaS and PaaS models. Then, we'll look at the different SQL database types available on Azure, followed by service tiers and performance levels. Finally, we will demonstrate how to create Azure SQL Database and how to connect to it.

The following topics will be covered in this chapter:

- Introduction to Azure SQL Database
- SQL Database (IaaS/PaaS)
- Azure SQL Database types
- Service tier types
- Creating Azure SQL Database
- Connecting to Azure SQL Database

Introduction to Azure SQL Database

A database is the most important component of many modern applications. Therefore, it is no surprise that we have two chapters where I will cover most of the important key points and best practices for using Azure SQL Database.

Azure SQL Database is a relational database as a service, which means it follows the **Platform as a Service (PaaS)** cloud service model, where you do not have to manage the underlying infrastructure, including networks, storage, servers, the virtualization layer, the operating system, middleware, or runtime. You only have to manage your databases and do not even have to think about patching and updating your servers.

Why Azure SQL Database?

Besides the reasons I've covered in the previous chapters as to why the cloud is always better than a traditional infrastructure, there are lots of other reasons for using Azure SQL Database. These include the following:

- **Scalability**: Azure SQL Database can be scaled according to your needs and usage. More information about this topic will be covered later in the chapter.
- **Online scaling**: No downtime is needed to scale your database size. For example, you can start your application with a size that fits it in the beginning, and Azure SQL Database can respond to the database's requirements by scaling whenever necessary without causing any downtime.
- **Hardcore monitoring**: Azure SQL Database provides built-in monitoring and alerting tools that can be used to identify potential problems and even recommend actions to be taken in order to fix an issue. Alerts can also be generated based on the monitoring metrics, so you can receive an alert that something has gone wrong according to the monitoring baseline that the user can define according to his needs.
- **Built-in intelligence**: One of the coolest features of Azure SQL Database is built-in intelligence. It helps to reduce the costs involved in running databases and increases the performance of the application that uses Azure SQL Database as a backend.
- **Intelligent threat detection**: This feature utilizes SQL Database auditing in order to detect any harmful attempts to access data. It simply provides alerts for any abnormal behaviors.
- **High availability**: Microsoft provides many ways to ensure that Azure SQL Database is highly available:
    - **Automatic backup**: To avoid any issues that might cause data loss, automatic backups are performed on SQL Databases (these include full, differential, and transaction log backups).
    - **Point in time restores**: Azure SQL Database can be recovered to any point-in-time within the automatic backup retention period.
    - **Active geo-replication**: If you have an application that needs to be accessed from across the globe, you can use active geo-replication to avoid facing a high load on the original SQL Database. Azure geo-replication will create four secondary databases for the original database, with read access.
    - **Failover groups**: This feature is designed to help customers to recover from databases in secondary regions if a disaster occurs in the region that the original database is stored in.

This is a sneak peek of Azure SQL Database's most common features.

SQL Database (IaaS/PaaS)

An SQL Database can be implemented in Azure in two ways:

- **Using Azure SQL Database**: This follows the PaaS model, and will be covered in this chapter and the next one
- **Using Azure VMs and building SQL on them**: This follows the IaaS model, and will be covered in more detail shortly

Azure SQL Database (PaaS)

Azure SQL Database is a relational database as a service, built and hosted on Azure. It minimizes the cost of managing and provisioning databases. Using this model will reduce the responsibility for managing the virtual machines that host SQL Server, the operating system, and even the SQL Server software.

This model eliminates concerns regarding upgrades, backups, and even the high availability of databases, because they are not your responsibility anymore. Moreover, you can add databases as you wish, whenever you want. Taking this into account, you will pay less in credits because in this scenario you will not pay for a VM with SQL installed on it, plus the license credits; you will only pay for the database you are using.

Scenarios that would fit Azure SQL Database

Azure SQL Database would be a best fit for the following scenarios:

- Cloud applications that need to be developed quickly
- Building a highly-available and auto-upgradable database that is recoverable in the event of disasters
- A database with less management needed for its OS and configuration
- Building a **Software as a Service (SaaS)** application
- If you want complete management of your SQL installation, but no worries about hardware

SQL on Azure VMs (IaaS)

This type of deployment of SQL Server is much more complicated than using Azure SQL Database, as a VM built on Azure and SQL Server built upon it requires more administration. Also, you can use whichever versions you want to use (2008 R2, 2012, 2014, 2016, 2017, and 2019), and whichever edition you need (Developer, Express, Web, Standard, or Enterprise).

Scenarios that would suit SQL on Azure VMs

The following scenarios would be the best fit for building SQL on Azure VMs:

- Migrating existing on-premises apps to Azure with minimal changes
- Having a SQL environment that you have full access to
- Needing databases of up to 64 TB storage, since Azure SQL Database can support only up to 4 TB
- Building hybrid applications with SQL Database as a backend

Azure SQL Database types

Azure SQL Database is available in three flavors:

- Elastic database pools
- Single databases
- Managed instances

Elastic database pools

Elastic database pools are a great solution for managing multiple databases and scaling their performance according to the databases' needs, which means it is a good fit for databases with unpredictable usage demands, and this leads to a saving on credits. Elastic database pools share performance across many databases, since all of these databases are built on a single Azure SQL Database server.

Single databases

Single databases are a good fit for a set of databases with predictable performance, where the required resources for the databases are predetermined.

SQL database managed instance

This type allows you to run SQL Server with all the features of Microsoft SQL Server Enterprise in the cloud without needing to manage Windows VMs. It offers all the functionalities of Azure SQL Enterprise on Azure with the PaaS solution.

Service tier types

At the time of writing, there are two types of service tiers:

- DTU service tiers
- vCore service tiers

DTU service tiers

At the time of writing, there are three DTU service tiers for Azure SQL Database: Basic, Standard, and Premium. All of these offer support for elastic database pools and single databases only, but not the SQL database managed instance. The performance of these tiers is expressed in **Database Transaction Units (DTUs)** for single databases, and **elastic Database Transaction Units (eDTUs)** for elastic database pools.

DTUs specify the performance for single databases, as they provide a specific amount of resources to that database.

On the other hand, eDTUs do not provide a dedicated set of resources for a database, as they share resources within a specific Azure SQL Server with all the databases which run that server.

For more information about DTUs and eDTUs, you can check out the following article: https://docs.microsoft.com/en-us/azure/sql-database/sql-database-what-is-a-dtu.

To calculate your required DTUs, especially when you are migrating an on-premises SQL Server database, you can use the Azure SQL DTU calculator, which can be accessed at the following link: http://dtucalculator.azurewebsites.net/.

The following is a table from Microsoft that illustrates the different tiers' performance levels for elastic database pools:

	Basic	Standard	Premium
Maximum storage size per database	2 GB	1 TB	1 TB
Maximum storage size per pool	156 GB	4 TB	4 TB
Maximum eDTUs per database	5	3,000	4,000
Maximum eDTUs per pool	1,600	3,000	4,000
Maximum number of databases per pool	500	500	100

The following illustrates the different tiers' performance levels for single databases:

	Basic	Standard	Premium
Maximum storage size	2 GB	1 TB	4 TB
Maximum DTUs	5	3,000	4,000

For a detailed comparison of performance levels for single and elastic database pools, you can check out the following link: https://docs.microsoft.com/en-us/azure/sql-database/sql-database-resource-limits-logical-server#single-database-storage-sizes-and-performance-levels.

vCore service tiers

At the time of writing, there are three vCore service tiers for Azure SQL Database:

- **General purpose**: This tier provides scalable compute and storage options with IOPs up to 7,000 and 5-10 ms latency.
- **Hyperscale**: At the time of writing, this service tier is in preview, and it provides on-demand scalable storage with 200,000 IOPS and 1.2 ms latency for data and 7,000 IOPS, 5-10 ms latency for logs.

- **Business critical**: This tier is designed for high transaction rates and high resiliency with 200,000 IOPS and 1-2 ms latency. Moreover, it provides the option to have enhanced availability by spreading replicas across availability zones within one region.

For all the vCore service tiers, you can specify one of the two compute generations that are supported by Azure at present, according to your scenario:

- **Gen4**: Provides up to 24 cores and memory up to 168 GB
- **Gen5**: Provides up to 80 cores and memory up to 408 GB

Creating an Azure SQL Database

In order to create an Azure SQL Database, you need to create an Azure SQL Server first:

1. Navigate to the Azure portal, then to **All services**, and search for SQL servers.
2. When you open **SQL servers**, a new blade pops up, and if there are any SQL Servers that you created earlier, they will be displayed here. But since no SQL Servers have been created so far, it will be blank, as shown in the following screenshot:

3. To create a new Azure SQL Database, click on **Add**.
4. Once you have clicked on **Add,** a new blade will be opened where you have to specify the following:
   - **Server name**: Specify a descriptive server name for the server, although the name you might provide will not be valid because it has been used before for another SQL Server in the `database.windows.net` domain.
   - **Server admin login**: Specify the SQL Server admin username.
   - **Password**: Specify a strong password for the SQL Server.
   - **Subscription**: Specify the subscription that will be charged for using this service.
   - **Resource group**: Specify the resource group in which this resource will exist.
   - **Location**: Select the nearest location to the service for which you are creating Azure SQL Server. For example, if you are going to use it for a web app, make sure they are in the same region, or if you are going to use it as a backend of an application hosted on-premises or somewhere else, it's recommended to use the nearest region.
   - **Allow Azure services to access server**: If you enable this option, you are allowing other Azure services to access this server.
   - **Advanced Threat Protection**: This is a unified security package for discovering and classifying sensitive data, surfacing, mitigating potential database vulnerabilities, and detecting anomalous activities that could indicate a threat to your database. If you want to use it, you can have a trial for 60 days, and then it is 15 USD/server/month:

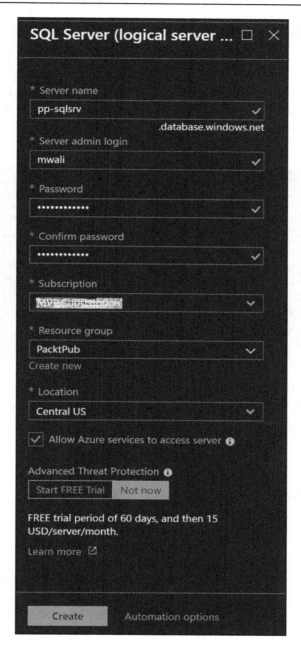

5. Once you are done, click on **Create** and the server will be created after few moments.

With SQL Server in place, you can now start to create the database by performing the following steps:

1. Navigate to the Azure portal, then to **All services**, and search for SQL database.
2. When you open **SQL databases**, a new blade pops up, and if there are any SQL Databases that you created earlier, they will be displayed here. But since no SQL Servers have been created so far, it will be blank, as shown in the following screenshot:

3. To create a new Azure SQL Database, click on **Add**.
4. A new blade will be opened where you have to specify the following:
   - **Database name**: A descriptive name for the database.
   - **Subscription**: Specify the subscription the SQL Server you have created earlier is using.
   - **Resource group**: Specify the resource group in which this database exists.
   - **Select source**: You can select one of the following as a source for the database:
     - **Blank database**: An empty database where you can create your own tables.
     - **Sample (AdventureWorksLT)**: You can use this option to have a sample database provided by Azure. If selected, it loads the **AdventureWorks** schema and data into your new database.
     - **Backup**: If you want to restore a previously backed-up Azure SQL Database to be used in this case.

- **Server**: Specify the SQL Server you want to build the database into. You can either select an existing one, such as the one we have just created, or create a new one, as shown in the following screenshot:

- **Want to use SQL elastic pools**: If you select **Not now**, it means this database will be a single database.
- **Pricing tier**: Choose a SQL service tier and performance level that best fits your application needs. There are two purchasing models:
  - **DTU-base model**: This consists of the DTU service tiers we discussed earlier (Basic, Standard, and Premium), where you can specify the DTUs and the size that can be used by the database:

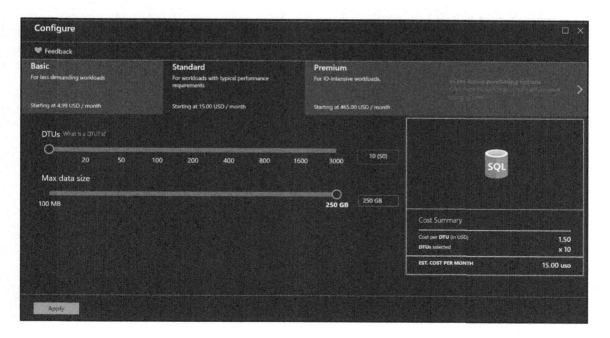

- **vCore-based model**: This is a more customizable model, where you can select compute and storage resources. Moreover, you can make use of Azure Hybrid Benefit for SQL Server to save costs:

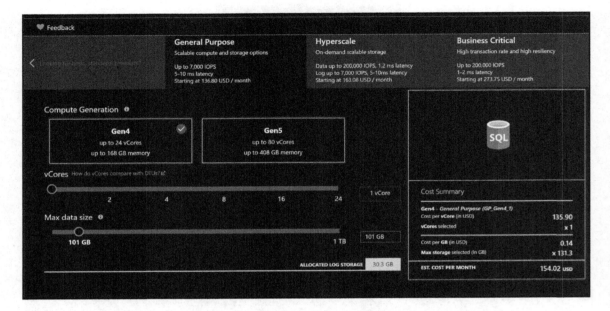

- **Collation**: Database collation defines the rules that sort and compare data, and cannot be changed after database creation. The default database collation is `SQL_Latin1_General_CP1_CI_AS`

5. Once you are ready, click on **Create**:

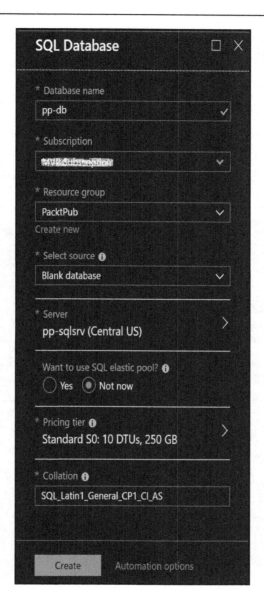

Connecting to Azure SQL Database

As mentioned earlier, when you create an Azure Database via the Azure portal, all Azure services will be allowed to access this database with no further configuration.

However, when you want to connect to the database from anywhere else, there is some configuration that needs to be done.

Server-level firewall

To allow access to Azure SQL Database from somewhere else, you will have to set a server-level firewall rule, as described in the following steps:

1. Navigate to the SQL Server and select **Firewalls and virtual networks**, as shown in the following screenshot:

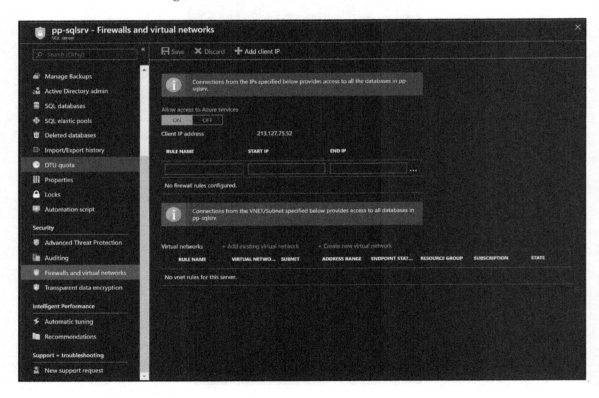

2. Then, you can specify the range of IP addresses you would like to allow access for, but if you want to specify a single IP address, you can add it as **START IP** and **END IP**. In this scenario, we will click on **Add client IP**, which will detect your own public IP address and add it, as shown in the following screenshot:

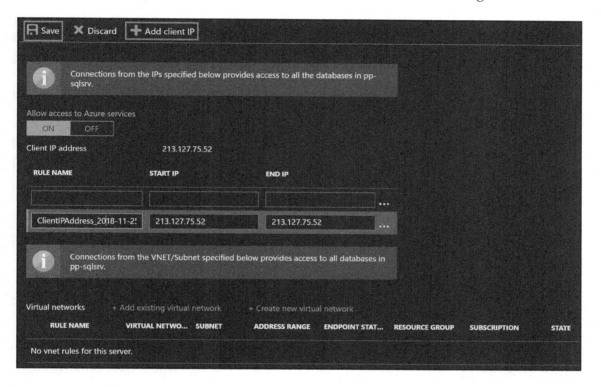

3. Once you are done, click on **Save**.
4. You can do the same thing on the level of the database by navigating to the database and clicking on **Set server firewall**, as shown in the following screenshot:

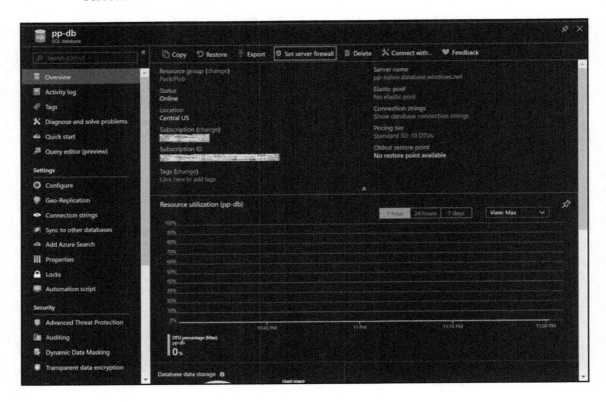

Make sure that port 1433 is open in your environment, which is used for communication between the SQL Server and the client (**SQL Server Management Studio (SSMS)**).

Connecting to Azure SQL Database using SQL SSMS

To connect to the created database via SSMS, you can follow these steps:

1. Navigate to the database blade and copy **Server name** from the overview page.

2. Open SSMS, paste the name of the server, change the **Authentication** to **SQL Server Authentication**, and enter the SQL Server credentials that you entered during SQL Server creation, as shown in the following screenshot:

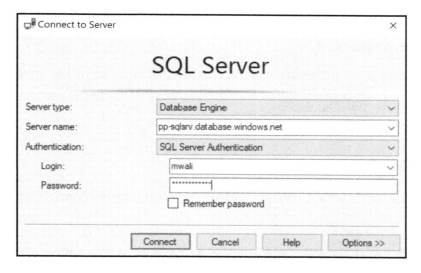

3. Once you click on **Connect**, you will be connected to your database on Azure, as shown in the following screenshot:

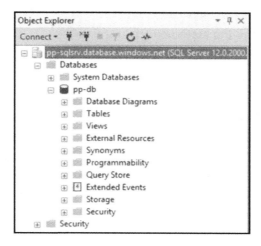

Summary

So far, we have gone through the basics of Azure SQL Database by understanding what it is, its types, and why we would use it.

Then, a creation for Azure SQL Database has been demonstrated with a guide about how to do it and how to connect to it.

In the next chapter, more information about Azure SQL Database will be covered about the other types, such as elastic pool and managed instance, providing a highly available solution with Azure SQL Database.

Questions

1. You can scale your databases with a very short interruption:
    - True
    - False
2. Which one of the following is not an Azure SQL Database type?
    - Elastic pool
    - Spanning databases
    - Single database
    - Managed instance
3. Which of the following statements is not true?
    - You can connect to an Azure SQL Database from an Azure VM without adding a firewall rule
    - If an Azure Web App is using Azure SQL Database as a backend, you will have to allow access to it by adding firewall rules for the IP addresses of the web app
    - You can connect to Azure SQL Database from another Azure subscription without adding firewall rules
    - In order to connect to Azure SQL Database from your personal computer, you need to add a firewall rule to allow access

Further reading

- *DTU-based service tiers* (`https://docs.microsoft.com/en-us/azure/sql-database/sql-database-service-tiers-dtu`)
- *Azure SQL Database purchasing models* (`https://docs.microsoft.com/en-us/azure/sql-database/sql-database-service-tiers`)
- *Prepay for SQL Database compute resources with Azure SQL Database reserved capacity* (`https://docs.microsoft.com/en-us/azure/sql-database/sql-database-reserved-capacity`)
- *Scale single database resources in Azure SQL Database* (`https://docs.microsoft.com/en-us/azure/sql-database/sql-database-single-database-scale`)

8
Managing Azure SQL Database

In this chapter, you will continue to learn about Azure SQL Database. We will cover how to work with Azure SQL elastic database pools, how to set Active Directory authentication in Azure SQL Database, the business continuity for Azure SQL Database, and how to work with an Azure SQL Managed Instance.

The following topics will be covered in this chapter:

- Azure SQL elastic database pools
- Azure AD authentication
- Azure SQL Database business continuity
- Azure SQL Managed Instances

Azure SQL elastic database pools

In the previous chapter, we gave you a sneak peek at elastic database pools. In this section, you will learn more about them, and you will work on creating and managing them.

Benefits of using elastic database pools

An elastic database pool can help you to achieve the following:

- Simplify performance management for multiple databases, especially when usage patterns are unpredictable
- Reduce the cost of multiple databases and provide a convenient way to control the budget
- Perfect choice for **Software as a service (SaaS)** apps that provision a single database per tenant, to get isolation benefits

It's not recommended to use elastic database pools for mission critical applications that require specific consumption and can be degraded by other databases running in the same pool.

Creating an elastic database pool

To get your elastic database pool up and running, follow these steps:

1. Navigate to the **SQL servers** blade and click on **New pool**, as shown in the following screenshot:

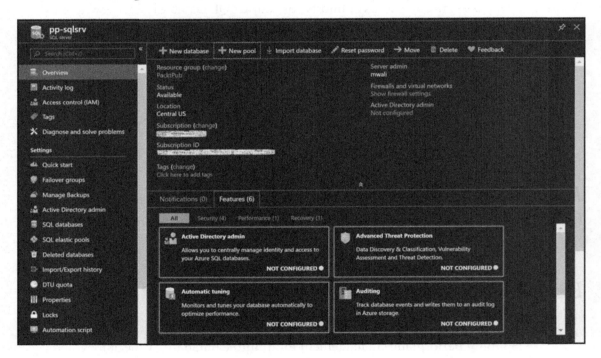

2. A new blade will open, and you will have to specify the following:
   - **Name**: Specify a descriptive name for the pool.
   - **Configure pool**: Specify a service tier:

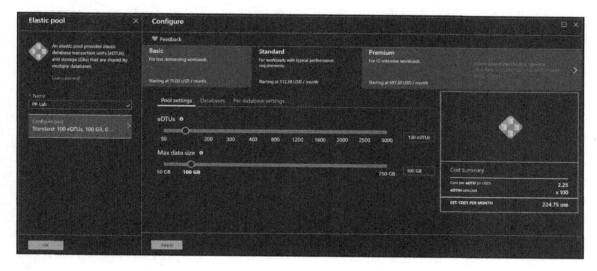

3. When you have finished, click on **OK**.

4. To view and manage the pool after its creation, navigate to **SQL elastic pools**, in the same blade of the SQL Server that you are creating the pool in:

Adding a database to an elastic pool

Once your elastic database pool is up and running, you can add databases to it; to do so, follow these steps:

1. Navigate to the SQL Server in which you created the pool.
2. Then, go to **SQL elastic pools** and click on the pool that you want to add databases to.

3. A new blade will open. In the **Overview** blade, click on **Create database**, as shown in the following screenshot:

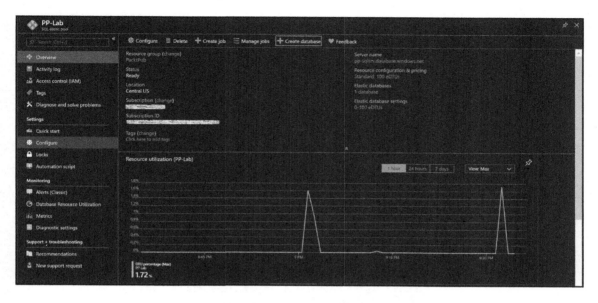

4. A new blade will open, where you will have to specify the following:
   - **Database name**: Provide a name for the database.
   - **Select source**: The source for the database.

- **Collation**: Database collation defines the rules that sort and compare data, and cannot be changed after database creation. The default database collation is `SQL_Latin1_General_CP1_CI_AS`:

5. When you are done, click on **OK**, and a new database will be created and added to the pool.

Setting Azure Active Directory authentication

So far, we have been using SQL authentication to connect to Azure SQL Database, as we did in the previous chapter, via SQL Server Management Studio. Using Azure **Active Directory** (**AD**) will provide centralized administration for database users' identities, providing the following benefits:

- Another method of SQL Server authentication
- Controlling the password change for a centralized location
- Assigning user permissions on the database level
- Support of token-based authentication for the applications that connect to the database
- Protection of user profiles across the database servers
- Avoidance of the need to store passwords, as you will be able to use different methods of authentication, which we will cover shortly

In the next chapter, Azure Active Directory will be covered in more detail.

To enable Azure AD authentication for Azure SQL Database, follow these steps:

1. Navigate to the Azure SQL Server that you want to enable this feature for.

2. Under **Settings**, click on **Active Directory admin**, as shown in the following screenshot:

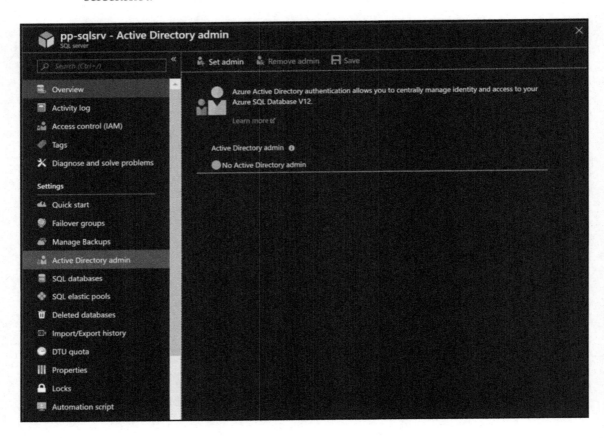

3. Click on **Set admin**, and a new blade will open, in which you can choose the AD user that you want to grant access to that SQL Server, as shown in the following screenshot:

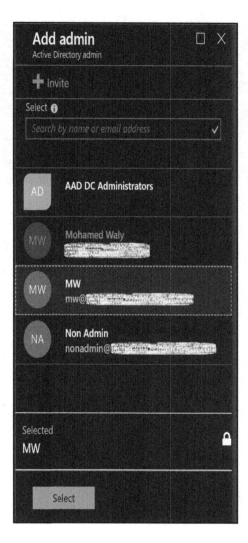

4. Once you are done, click on **Save**:

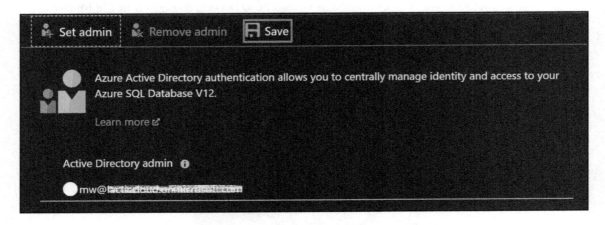

5. If you want to connect to Azure SQL Database using your Azure AD user, you can select one of the following authentication methods:

- **Active Directory - Universal with MFA support**: You can use this option if MFA is enabled for the AD user that you will be logging in with.
- **Active Directory - Password**: With this option, you can set the AD user and password manually, in the SSMS.
- **Active Directory - Integrated**: This option should be used if you are logged into the machine using your Azure AD user, and you will not have to enter the username and password to log in, as the credentials that you used to log into the machine will be considered.

The following screenshot depicts the **Active Directory – Password** option:

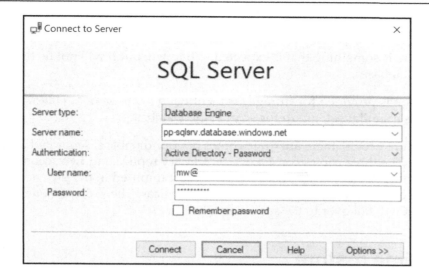

If you have an SQL Server running on an Azure VM, you cannot do it using an Azure AD account, but the domain AD account is supported.

Azure SQL Database business continuity

You now have your database up and running in the cloud, and you can even connect to it, and create, delete, and update the tables as you wish.

In this section, you will learn how to build a highly available and business continuity database.

How business continuity works in Azure SQL Database

Microsoft does its best to address any issues that may occur in Azure SQL Database, and it provides solutions to the following issues.

Hardware failure

Hardware failure is something that is expected to happen, but it will not be the reason that you lose your databases.

Just as replication is provided for storage (as mentioned in Chapter 2, *Understanding Azure Storage*), there is a similar safeguard for Azure SQL Databases.

If hardware failure occurs, there are three copies of your database, separated across three physical nodes. The three copies consist of one primary replica and two secondary replicas, and, to avoid any data loss, write operations are not committed in the primary replica until they have been committed to one of the secondary replicas. Therefore, whenever hardware failure occurs, it will fail over to the secondary replica.

Point-in-time restore

To avoid any issues that might cause data loss, automatic backups are performed on SQL databases (these include full, differential, and transaction log backups).

Azure SQL Database can be recovered to any point in time, within the automatic backup retention period.

The retention period varies from one tier to another: seven days for the Basic tier, 35 days for the Standard tier, and 35 days for the Premium tier. This solution would suit a scenario in which your database has been corrupted and you want to restore it to the last healthy point.

To restore your database to the last healthy point, you have to follow these steps:

1. Navigate to the database that you want to restore to the last healthy point, and click on **Restore**, as shown in the following screenshot:

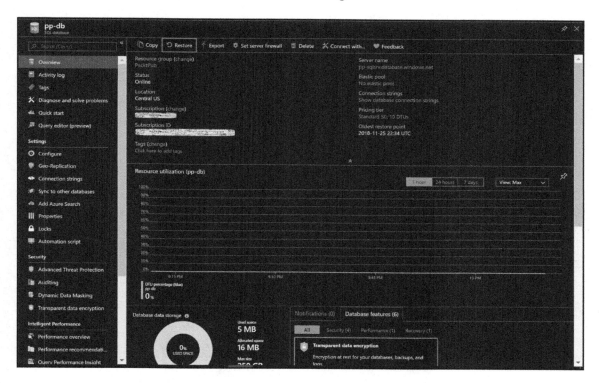

2. Once you have clicked on **Restore**, a new blade will pop up, where you can provide the restored database with a new database name, determine the time that you want to restore to, and change the pricing tier for the restored database, as shown in the following screenshot:

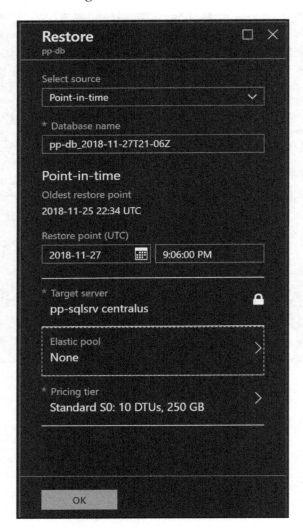

3. When you click on **OK**, the database will start to be restored.

Point-in-time restoration key points

The following key points provide more information about point-in-time restoration:

- When you restore a database, a new database is created, which means that you will have to pay for the new database, too.
- You cannot provide the new database with the same name as the original database, because the original still exists; to do so, you would have to remove the original one.
- You can choose a restoration point between the earliest point and the latest backup time, which is six minutes before the current time.
- The database recovery time varies from one database to another, according to many factors; some of them are as follows:
  - The database's size
  - The number of transaction logs involved in the operations
  - The database's performance level
  - If you are restoring the database from a different region, the network bandwidth might cause a delay

Restoring a deleted database

You can accidentally remove a database, or you might remove a database and figure out that you still need it later on. This can be a tough situation. However, Microsoft Azure supports database recovery, even in the case of deletion. (The SQL Server on which the database was built cannot have been deleted; at the time of writing this book, there was no support for the recovery of deleted SQL Servers.)

To restore a deleted database, follow these steps:

1. Navigate to SQL Servers and select the server in which the deleted database was built.
2. Scroll down to **Deleted databases** in the **SQL server** blade, as shown in the following screenshot:

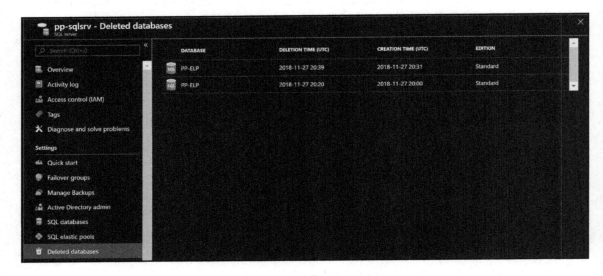

3. Select the database that you want to restore, and name it as you wish, considering that you cannot provide the name of an existing database that is already running on the same SQL Server (but you can give it its old name), as shown in the following screenshot:

4. Once you are done, click on **OK**, and it will start the restoration process.

Active geo-replication

Active geo-replication is one of the most important business continuity methodologies.

When using active geo-replication, you can configure up to four secondary databases within the same region, or in different regions with reading access. This will help to reduce latency for users or applications that need to query the database from different regions.

If a catastrophic disaster occurs, you can fail over to the other region by using a failover group. Failover groups are mainly designed to manage every aspect of geo-replication automatically, such as connectivity, relationships, and failover. Provided it is available for all databases in respective service tiers in all the regions.

To implement active geo-replication, follow these steps:

1. Navigate to the desired database in the Azure portal and click on **Geo-Replication**, under **Settings**, as shown in the following screenshot:

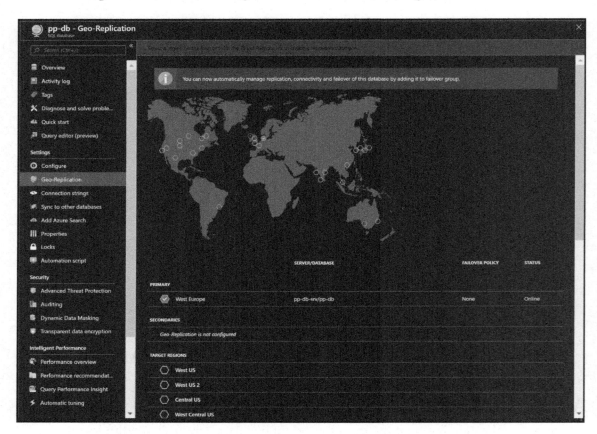

2. Click on the region that you want to replicate to, as shown in the following screenshot:

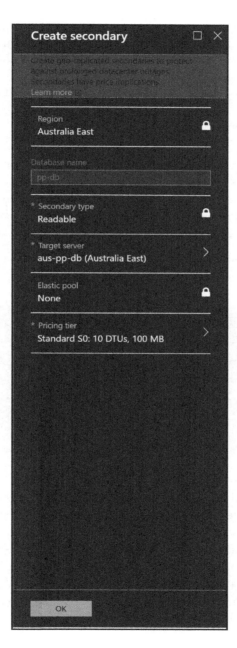

3. Once the region has been selected, a new blade will pop up, asking you to configure the secondary server for which the database will be replicated; you will have to specify the following:

- **Target server**: If you have not created another Azure SQL Server in that region to act as a secondary server, you can click on **Target server** and go through the wizard for creating a new SQL Server (or select an existing one, if you have already created it).
- **Pricing tier**: Select a pricing tier that is not lower that the original one.

4. Once you are done, click on **OK**.

Auto-failover groups

Auto-failover groups make good use of active geo-replication by providing group-level replication and automatic failover. Moreover, you will not have to change the SQL connection string if a failover occurs. To create an auto-failover group, follow these steps:

1. Navigate to the SQL Server in which the databases exist.
2. Under **Settings**, click on **Failover groups**, as shown in the following screenshot:

3. Click on **Add group** to add an auto-failover group.
4. A new blade will pop up, where you will have to specify the following:

- **Failover group name**: Specify a descriptive name for the failover group.
- **Secondary server**: Specify the secondary server that will host the replicated database.
- **Read/Write failover policy**: You can let this process be done automatically, which is the default, and is recommended. Otherwise, you will have to do it manually.

- **Read/Write grace period (hours)**: Specify the time between every automatic failover.
- **Database within the group**: Select the databases in that Azure SQL Server that you would like to add to the auto-failover group:

5. Once you are done, click on **Create**.

Azure SQL Managed Instances

In the previous chapter, Azure SQL Managed Instances were introduced as one of the Azure SQL Database types. In this section, we will provide more information on them.

Azure SQL Managed Instances offer the full functionalities of SQL Server Enterprise. If you need some features that were not available in the previous types that we discussed (such as SQL Agent or linked servers), this type will fulfill your needs.

Azure SQL Managed Instances can be better than the other Azure SQL Database types, for the following reasons:

- **SQL Server Enterprise edition features support**: All of the features that you used to work with an SQL Server on-premises can be used with this type.
- **Dedicated instance**: Unlike with the other types of Azure SQL Databases, you will not be sharing the server on which you run your database with others.
- **Backward compatibility**: If you have legacy versions of SQL Servers on-premises, you can migrate the databases to Azure SQL Managed Instances with no problems. Notice that you cannot migrate versions earlier than SQL Server 2005.

Azure SQL Managed Instance types

The following are the two types of Azure SQL Managed Instance:

- **General purpose**: This type is meant for applications with no high tech requirements for performance and I/O latency
- **Business critical**: This type is meant for applications that need high Input/Output Operations Per Second and high stability during the maintenance of the instance

Creating an Azure SQL Managed Instance

Creating an Azure SQL Managed Instance is a straightforward process; all you need to do is follow these steps:

1. Navigate to **All services** and search for `SQL managed instance`; fill in the following fields:

2. Click on it, and a new blade will open; click on **Add**, and a new blade will open, where you have to specify the following:

   - **Subscription**: Specify the subscription that will be charged for using this service
   - **Managed instance name**: Specify a descriptive name for the managed instance
   - **Managed instance admin login**: Specify the admin of the managed instance
   - **Password**: Specify a strong password for the managed instance
   - **Location**: Select the nearest region to the service/application that will work with the managed instance.
   - **Virtual network**: You have two options, as follows:
     - **Create a new virtual network**: This option will create a new virtual network, compliant with the rules required for the SQL Managed Instance.
     - Select one of the virtual networks/subnets that you already have.
   - **Resource group**: Select the resource group in which it will exist as a resource.
   - **Pricing tier**: Select one of the types that were covered in the previous section, in order to fulfill the needs of your applications. You also need to set the number of vCores and the storage size that you need. It supports two compute generations, as follows:
     - **Gen 4**: Based on Intel E5-2673 v3 (Haswell) 2.4 GHz processors, this generation supports 8/16/24 vCores and storage ranging from 32 GB to 8 TB.
     - **Gen 5**: Based on Intel E5-2673 v4 (Broadwell) 2.3 GHz processors, this generation supports 8/16/24/32/40/64/80 vCores and storage ranging from 32 GB to 4 TB.

3. Once you are done, click on **Create**:

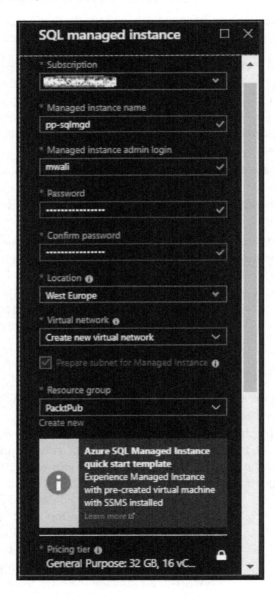

Connecting to an Azure SQL Managed Instance

Connecting to the SQL Managed Instance can be done by using SQL Server Management Studio, but only under the following conditions:

- You are trying to connect to the server from an Azure VM that exists in the same VNet as the SQL Managed Instance.
- You are connecting from an Azure VM that does not share the same VNet as the Managed Instance; you need to make sure that it has network connectivity to the VNet where the Managed Instance exists (via a VNet peering, for example).
- You can connect from on-premises, but with a network connection in place between your on-premises and Azure, via one of the following options:
  - Point-to-site VPN connection
  - Site-to-site VPN connection
  - Express route

When you have achieved one of the preceding conditions, you can run SSMS and connect to the Managed Instance in the same way that you did in the previous chapter.

Azure SQL Managed Instance key points

The following key points will provide more insight into Azure SQL Managed Instances:

- If you are planning to use a precreated subnet for the SQL Managed Instance when you create it, ensure that the following conditions are met:
  - It is not a gateway subnet
  - There are not any service endpoints enabled for it
  - The subnet is not used by any other service
  - At least 16 IP addresses are available in the subnet
- **Prepare subnet for managed instance** is an option during the SQL Managed Instance creation, and it will handle the following:
  - It will create a user-defined table for the subnet 0.0.0.0/0 next-hop internet
  - A network security group will be created with some security rules, to be compliant with the Managed Instance deployment requirements

- When you increase the storage size in the **Pricing tier** blade, the custom amount to the nearest value divided by 32 would be rounded.
- You can make use of the hybrid use benefit and reuse an SQL Server license, saving up to 55% off the Managed Instance costs.

 You can configure a VNet for Azure SQL Database Managed Instance at `https://docs.microsoft.com/en-us/azure/sql-database/sql-database-managed-instance-vnet-configuration`.

Summary

By now, most of the important topics about Azure SQL Database have been covered. In this chapter, we covered more information about Azure SQL elastic database pools and Azure SQL Managed Instance. In addition, we discussed enabling AD authentication, which will help you to have well-managed, secure authentication to databases. We also discussed some solutions that will allow for business continuity.

In the next chapter, we will go over Azure AD, and you will learn how to manage identities in the cloud.

Questions

1. You cannot create an empty SQL elastic pool:
   - True
   - False

2. Which of the following is not an AD authentication method for Azure SQL Database?
   - **Active Directory - Password**
   - **Active Directory - SSPR**
   - **Active Directory - Integrated**
   - **Active Directory - Universal with MFA Support**

3. Which of the following statements is not true?
   - The database's size is not important during database recovery
   - The database's performance level is important during database recovery
   - The number of transaction logs involved in the operations is important during database recovery

4. List the conditions required for the subnet in which the Azure SQL Managed Instance will be created.

Further reading

- *How do I choose the correct pool size* (https://docs.microsoft.com/en-us/azure/sql-database/sql-database-elastic-pool#how-do-i-choose-the-correct-pool-size)
- *Create contained database users in your database mapped to Azure AD identities* (https://docs.microsoft.com/en-us/azure/sql-database/sql-database-aad-authentication-configure#create-contained-database-users-in-your-database-mapped-to-azure-ad-identities)
- *Use Azure Active Directory Authentication for authentication with SQL* (https://docs.microsoft.com/en-us/azure/sql-database/sql-database-aad-authentication)
- *Configuring a Custom DNS for Azure SQL Database Managed Instance* (https://docs.microsoft.com/en-us/azure/sql-database/sql-database-managed-instance-custom-dns
- *Azure SQL Database Managed Instance Connectivity Architecture* (https://docs.microsoft.com/en-us/azure/sql-database/sql-database-managed-instance-connectivity-architecture)

Understanding Azure Active Directory

9

In this chapter, you will be introduced to the most well known identity management solution, Active Directory, but as a service provided on Azure. You will understand the difference between Azure AD and on-premises AD, its benefits, and the difference between its different flavors. Then, you will get your hands dirty by learning how to work with Azure AD users and groups. Finally, you will learn some of the most commonly used aspects of Azure AD, such as self-service password reset, users sign-in activities, multi-factor authentication, and adding custom domain names.

The following topics will be covered:

- Introduction to Azure AD
- Working with users in Azure AD
- Working with groups in Azure AD
- Azure AD common tasks

Introduction to Azure AD

Identity has always played a vital role in IT environments in the last 20 years. With the new era of cloud, identity continues to play a central role.

For a long time, on-premises AD was the most used identity management application and Microsoft is working on extending it to the cloud; that is why Azure AD was offered.

Back in 2012, Microsoft announced Azure AD with some humble features. Since then, many features have been added to Azure AD to make it more mature.

Azure AD is a fully managed multi-tenant service by Microsoft that offers access and an identity management service.

However, Azure AD is not a total replacement for Windows Server Active Directory. For instance, you cannot assign group policies to users and computers, and objects, such as faxes and printers, using Azure AD. On the other hand, Azure AD can be considered a centralized location for Microsoft cloud applications, such as Office 365, Microsoft Intune, Dynamics 365, and so on.

That's why if you want to have the best experience, it is recommended to use Azure AD and Windows Server AD. This hybrid model will not only give you the full functionalities of Windows Server but also the features of Azure AD.

Azure AD benefits

Azure AD comes with many benefits, such as the following:

- **Single sign-on (SSO)**: It provides the ability to access multiple applications in easier and faster ways. Moreover, it grants access for new employees, and terminates it for leavers. As a result, you will be compliant with the identity and security protocols.
- **SaaS solution**: You do not have to implement and manage servers for AD as you used to do on-premises. However, you have a highly available, scalable solution that is just ready to use.
- **Integration with Windows Server AD**: It supports the integration with Windows Server AD, with a complimentary solution. For example, SSO can be used for users in to provide a seamless model, whether you are working in the office or remotely.
- **Integration with other cloud services**: It integrates not only with Windows Server AD but also with other cloud services, such as Office 365, Dynamics 365, and Sales force.
- **Multi-factor authentication (MFA) support**: It provides an MFA, which improves the security against identity violation.
- **Global presence**: Azure AD in many Azure regions across the globe provides a good service wherever you are.
- **Less risk**: It will detect unusual user behaviors and will automatically respond to them.
- **Application proxy**: It will leverage the SSO to provide a secure remote web access to on-premises-based web apps, without having to establish a VPN connection.
- **Domain Join**: Windows 10 based devices can join Azure AD without the need to join Windows Server AD.

Azure AD flavors

Azure AD is available in four flavors at the time of writing.

Free

This is the lowest tier of Azure AD editions and whenever you sign up for any of the Microsoft cloud services, this will be on offer. It has some of the Azure AD features that will help you to get started, but for sure you will need more when you recognize the benefits you can get when you have higher flavors. This flavor offers such features as SSO, B2B collaboration, self-service password change for cloud users, security/usage reports, and domain join for Windows 10 and AD connect, which offers integration with Windows Server AD.

Basic

On top of what is supported for the free tier, this tier provides the following services:

- Group-based access management/provisioning
- Self-service password reset
- Company branding (logon pages/access panel customization)
- Application proxy
- 99.9% SLA

Premium P1

This tier supports what is supported in the basic tier, plus the following:

- Advanced group features
- Self-service password reset/change/unlock with on-premises write-back
- Device objects two-way synchronization between on-premises directories and Azure AD (device write-back)
- MFA
- Microsoft Identity Manager User Client Access License
- Cloud App Discovery
- Connect Health
- Automatic password rollover for group accounts
- Conditional access

- Third-party identity governance partner integration
- Terms of use
- SharePoint Limited Access
- OneDrive for Business Limited Access
- Third-party MFA partner integration
- Microsoft Cloud App Security integration

Premium P2

This tier supports what is supported in the Premium P1, plus the following:

- Identity protection
- Privileged identity management
- Access reviews

 These features are enhanced regularly, and Microsoft keeps adding new features. You can check the following link for more information about Azure AD flavors: https://azure.microsoft.com/en-us/pricing/ details/active-directory/.

Working with users in Azure AD

In this section, you will learn how to do some elementary tasks with Azure AD users.

Creating an Azure AD user

In order to create an Azure AD user, you need to perform the following steps:

1. Navigate to the Azure portal, go to **All services,** and search Azure Active Directory:

2. When you click on it, a new blade will be opened where you can have an overview about the current Azure AD tenant that was created when you first created your subscription on Azure:

3. Navigate to **Users**, which is located under **Manager**, and a new blade will be opened displaying the current Azure AD users you have:

4. Click on **New user**, and a new blade will be opened where you have to fill in the following fields:

- **Name**: Specify the name of the user.
- **User name**: This is the identifier that the user enters to sign in to Azure AD according to the company's standards. For example, `mohamed@lacticcloud.com`.
- **Profile**: This is the address book information for the user. When you click on it, a new blade will be opened where you have to specify the following:

  - **First name**
  - **Last name**
  - **Job title**
  - **Department**

- **Properties**: This will help you to specify the source of authority. For example, if it is Azure AD or Windows Server AD.

- **Groups**: When you click on this, a new blade will be opened where you can select the groups for which you want that user to be a part of:

- **Directory role**: This is where you specify the admin type you want to assign to the user. When you click on it, a new blade will be opened where you have to select one of the following types:
    - **User**: Normal user that can access only the resources assigned to him.
    - **Global administrator**: This is a user with full control over all directory resources.

- **Limited administrator**: This is a user with admin privileges for some services in Azure and is identified according to the current available roles, such as an application administrator who can create and manage all aspects of registrations and enterprise apps

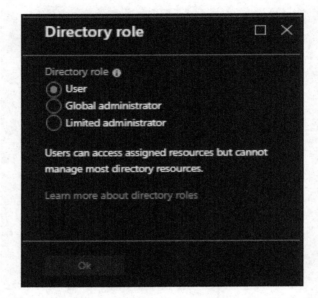

- **Password**: A temporary password is assigned to the user that you can view by clicking on **Show password** to share it with the user and once he/she logs in, he/she will be asked to change the password:

5. Once you are done with filling in the fields, click on **Create** and the user will be created within a moment.

 For more information about the application roles, check the following article: `https://docs.microsoft.com/en-us/azure/active-directory/users-groups-roles/directory-assign-admin-roles`.

User password reset

Resetting Azure AD user passwords is a very straightforward process. You need to perform the following steps:

1. Navigate to **Azure Active Directory** | **Users** and select the user you want to reset the password for.

2. Click on **Reset password**:

3. A new blade will be opened, informing you that if you reset the password, a temporary password will be assigned and the user will be prompted to change the password in the next sign in. To proceed, just click on **Reset password**:

4. A temporary password will be assigned, and you can copy it and share it with the user:

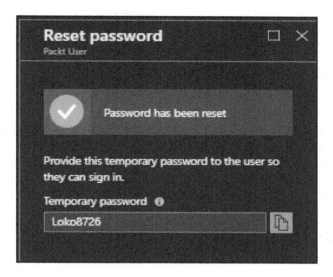

Deleted users

By default, when an Azure AD user is deleted, it will not be gone for good. However, it will be moved to another blade called **Deleted users** and it will be stored there for 30 days before being permanently deleted.

To restore users, perform the following steps:

1. Navigate to **Azure Active Directory** | **Users** | **Deleted users**.
2. Select the users you want to restore, and click on **Restore user**:

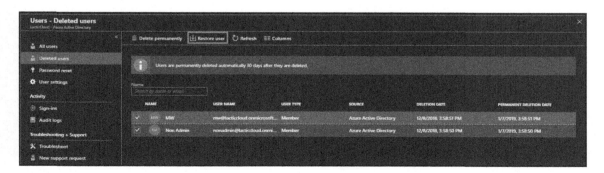

3. You will be prompted to confirm your desire to restore the users:

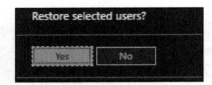

4. Once you click on **Yes**, they will be restored.

 If you want to permanently delete a deleted user, you have to go through the same process, but instead of clicking on **Restore user**, click on **Delete permanently**.

Working with groups in Azure AD

For a better organization for your environment, you should use Azure AD groups. In this section, you will learn how to work with Azure AD groups.

Creating an Azure AD group

To create and Azure AD group, perform the following steps:

1. Navigate to **Azure Active Directory** | **Groups**.
2. A new blade will be opened. Click on **New group**, as shown in the following screenshot:

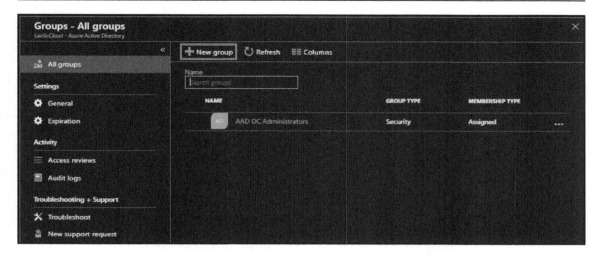

3. A new blade will open, where you have to specify the following:
    - **Group type**: Like the group types in Windows Server Active Directories, there's two types of group for Azure AD:
        - **Security**: This acts the same as the on-premises security group. It's used for security purposes, where you can add users or computers to the group and assign permissions to the group to have access to specific resources.
        - **Office 365**: This acts the same as the on-premises distribution group. It's used for collaboration purposes, where you can give the group users access to calendars, shared mailboxes, and much more.
    - **Group name**: Specify a descriptive name for the group.
    - **Group description**: Specify a short description for the group. However, it's not mandatory.

- **Membership type**: There are three membership types:
  - **Assigned**: You can specify which users/groups you would like to add to the group, as shown in the following screenshot:

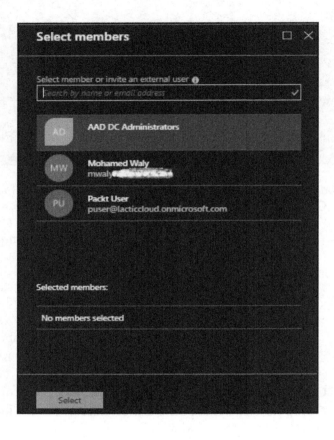

- **Dynamic user**: You can add dynamic rules to add or remove users from the group according to their compliance with the rules, as shown in the following screenshot:

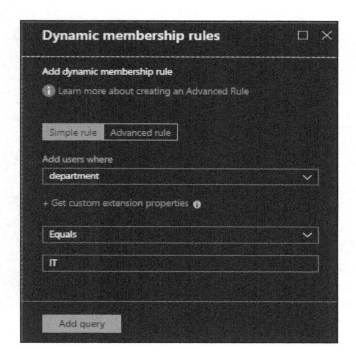

- **Dynamic device**: This is the same as the dynamic users, except it is used for devices:

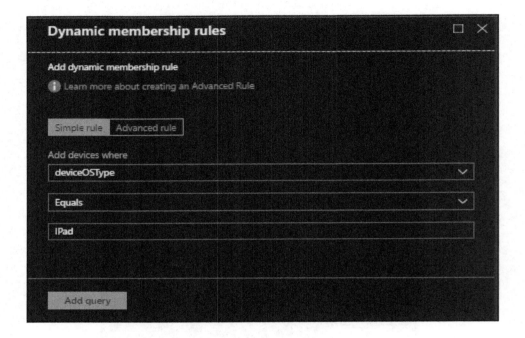

4. Once you are done, click on **Create**:

There are two types of dynamic rules:

- **Simple rule**: This is where you can specify the conditions by selecting the property, operator, and value from a drop-down list, as you saw earlier.
- **Advanced rule**: This is where you can write specific syntax for the rules you want to implement. You can check more information about the syntax from the following link: `https://docs.microsoft.com/en-us/azure/active-directory/users-groups-roles/groups-dynamic-membership`.

Azure AD common tasks

In this section, we will go through the configuration of the common tasks of Azure AD.

Self-service password reset

Self-service password reset is one of the coolest features that saves a great deal of time for the IT admins by allowing the users themselves to reset their own passwords.

In order to configure this feature, perform the following steps:

1. Navigate to **Azure Active Directory** | **Users** | **Password reset**.
2. A new blade will be opened displaying the current properties of the self-service password. It displays three statuses for the password reset:
    - **None**: This is the disabled state of the self-service password reset.
    - **Selected**: This specifies the groups you want to enable this feature for.
    - **All**: This enables it for all Azure AD users:

3. Then, navigate to the **Authentication methods** blade, where you can specify the following:

- The number of methods required to reset, where you can define the number of alternate methods of identification a user in this directory must have to reset their password.
- The methods that are available to users. At the time of writing, the following methods can be used to reset the password:
  - **Mobile app notification (preview)**
  - **Mobile app code (preview)**
  - **Email**
  - **Mobile phone**
  - **Office phone**
  - **Security questions**

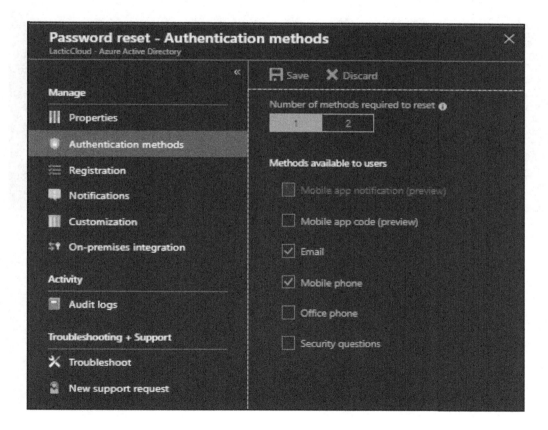

4. After that, navigate to the next blade, **Registration**, where you can require users to register when signing in or not and this designates whether unregistered users are prompted to register their own authentication information when they sign in for the first time. If set to **No**, administrators must manually specify the necessary password reset authentication information in the properties for each user in this directory, or instruct users to go to the registration portal URL directly. If you selected **Yes**, you need to define the period of time before registered users are prompted to re-confirm their existing authentication information is still valid, up to a maximum of 730 days. If set to 0 days, registered users will never be prompted to reconfirm their existing authentication information:

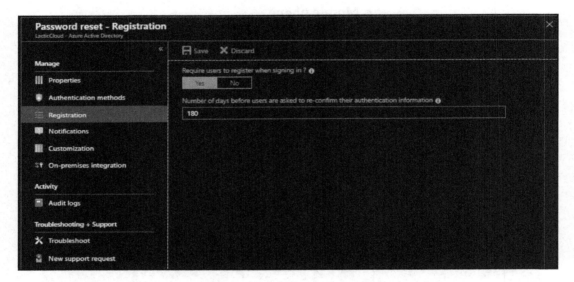

5. The next step is to set the notifications for password reset by selecting whether you want to notify the users when their password is reset by sending an email to their primary and alternative email address, and the same goes for admins if admins reset their password:

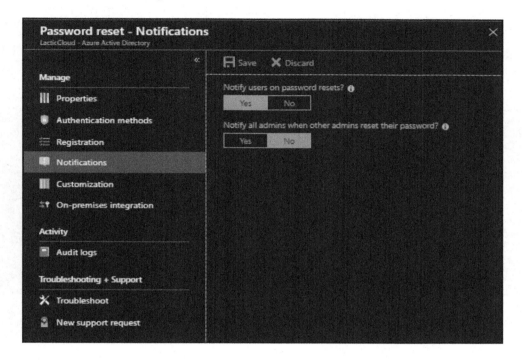

6. The further options are to customize the help desk contacts in the **Customization** and to configure this feature for hybrid scenarios, but this is not covered in this book.

Azure AD user sign-in activities

With Azure AD you can have more insights into the users sign-in activities and information about the managed application usage. But only the interactive sign-ins (in other words, only the manual logons) would be recorded and displayed but the non-interactive ones, such as the service-to-service authentication, will not be displayed.

To get this report, perform the following steps:

1. Navigate to **Azure Active Directory** | **Users** | **Sign-ins**:

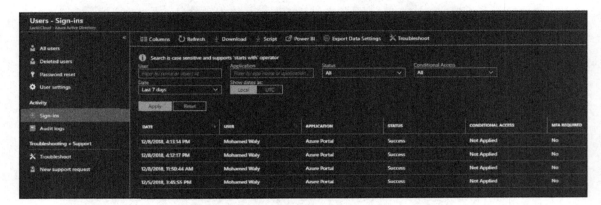

2. You can download this report as a CSV file by clicking on **Download** or clicking on **Script**, which will download a PowerShell script that can download a CSV file with the current columns by running it. You can remove some columns and add others by clicking on **Columns**, which will display more results, as shown in the following screenshot:

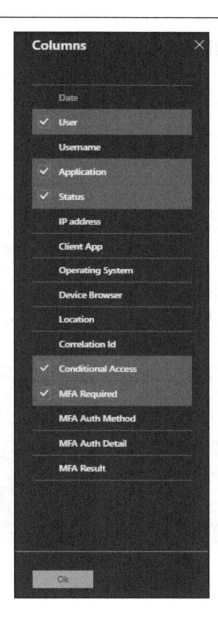

Multi-Factor Authentication

Multi-Factor Authentication is a multi-step verification to set challenges for attackers who might manage to get the user password. He will be asked to provide at least another proof of authentication, such as a phone call or SMS.

There are three ways to enable MFA:

- Changing User State: This option is a two steps verification every time the user will try to sign in. This is the type we are going to use as demo.
- Azure AD Identity Protection: This option would make use of the risk policy of Azure AD identity protection to enable the two steps verification. Providing that it will be done only based on the sign-in risk for all cloud applications.
- Conditional Access: This option make use of the conditional access policies where you have to specify the verification steps using a conditional access policy.

To enable it for Azure AD users, perform the following steps:

1. Navigate to **Azure Active Directory** | **Users** | **All users**.
2. Click on **Multi-Factor Authentication**, as shown in the following screenshot:

3. A new page will be opened where you can select the users you want to enable this feature for by selecting them and clicking on **Enable**, as shown in the following screenshot:

4. If you want to do it for a bulk of users, you can click on **bulk update**, which will ask you to upload a CSV file with the AD users in a specific format and enable MFA for all of them at once. To do this, you can download a sample CSV file to check the format of the users; you have to insert to the CSV file when you click on **bulk update**, as shown in the following screenshot:

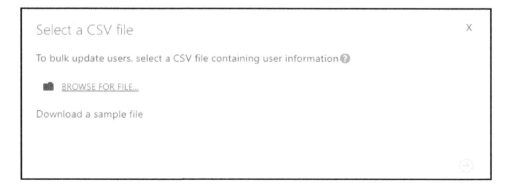

5. When you specify the users that you want to enable MFA for, you will be asked to confirm it, as shown in the following screenshot:

Configuring a custom domain name in Azure AD

When you use Azure AD, one of the first that will come to mind is to change the domain from `yourdomain.onmicrosoft.com` to `yourdomain.com`.

Adding custom domain names to Azure AD is an easy process. In order to do so, perform the following steps:

1. Navigate to **Azure Active Directory | Custom domain names**.
2. Click on **Add custom domain**, as shown in the following screenshot:

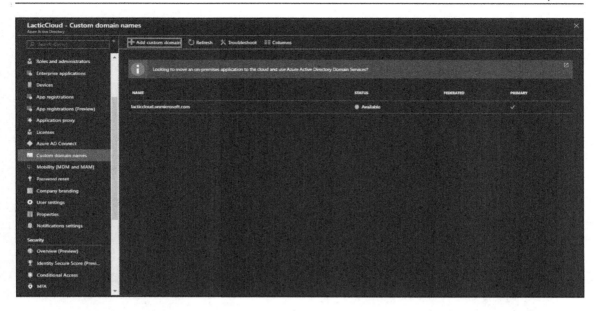

3. A new blade will be opened where you can add your public domain, as shown in the following screenshot:

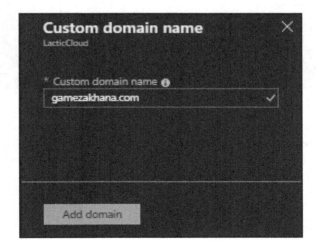

4. Once you click on **Add domain**, the domain will be added and you will be navigated to another blade where you can see the record values you need to add in your domain name registrar:

5. Navigate to your domain registrar and add the text record, and then come back to this blade and click **Verify**. This might take some time to propagate. Otherwise, the domain will be added to Azure AD custom domain names but will stay **Unverified** and you will not be able to use it.

Summary

So far, you have been introduced to Azure AD and how to get started with it. Azure AD is much more than what has been covered so far, yet it is a good start to working with Azure AD and, from here, you can continue to dig deeper and learn more about Azure AD.

Questions

1. Which of the following is not an Azure AD advantage:
    - SSO
    - Application proxy
    - Hybrid solution
    - Support for domain join for different OSes

2. When you delete an Azure AD user, he/she will be deleted permanently after __
    - 30 days
    - 42 days
    - 21 days

3. Custom domain names can be added to Azure AD even if you do not really own them. However, they will not be verified until you add the text record in your domain registrar.
    - True
    - False

Further reading

- *What is Azure Active Directory?* (https://docs.microsoft.com/en-us/azure/active-directory/fundamentals/active-directory-whatis)
- *What is guest user access in Azure Active Directory B2B?* (https://docs.microsoft.com/en-us/azure/active-directory/b2b/what-is-b2b)
- *What is Azure Active Directory B2C?* (https://docs.microsoft.com/en-us/azure/active-directory-b2c/active-directory-b2c-overview)
- *What is hybrid identity?* (https://docs.microsoft.com/en-us/azure/active-directory/hybrid/whatis-hybrid-identity?context=azure%2Factive-directory%2Fusers-groups-roles%2Fcontext%2Fugr-context)
- *Add branding to your organization's Azure Active Directory sign-in page* (https://docs.microsoft.com/en-us/azure/active-directory/fundamentals/customize-branding?context=azure/active-directory/users-groups-roles/context/ugr-context)

10
Monitoring and Automating Azure Services Using OMS

In this chapter, you will be introduced to **Operations Management Suite (OMS)** and its components. Then, we will go through Azure Log Analytics and how to work with it. Also, you will be introduced to Azure Automation and how to get started with it.

The following topics will be covered in this chapter:

- Introduction to OMS
- Introduction to Azure Log Analytics
- Onboarding OMS agents
- Azure Automation

Introduction to OMS

OMS is a cloud-based IT management solution that can be used to manage, monitor, protect, and automate your infrastructure either on the cloud or on-premises. It is a complementary solution for system center and, with both of them, you can have a fully integrated management solution, giving you the best hybrid experience ever.

OMS is a management as a service solution offered as one of Microsoft's cloud solutions to provide the customers with the following features:

- **Log Analytics**: This is the monitoring solution that collects, corresponds with, and searches the logs and acts accordingly, giving real-time operational insights and data analytics via visualized dashboards about what is monitored and its current status.
- **Automation**: Using Hybrid Runbook Worker, you can automate repetitive tasks , whether they be on-premises or cloud, either by PowerShell scripts or GUI runbooks.

- **Security and compliance**: Solutions for security and compliance help to identify, assess, and mitigate risks for the servers, providing higher protection to your workloads.
- **Recovery services (backup and disaster recovery)**: This feature provides you with a disaster recovery and business continuity solution. You can protect your VMs either in the cloud or on-premises. You can even protect your physical servers by backing them up to avoid the ransomware attacks. You can recover them with minimum data loss and provide business continuity by having them stored on Azure Site Recovery, ready to run on Azure whenever you have downtime.

OMS terminologies

The following terminologies will give you a better understanding about OMS, and they will be used throughout the chapter:

- **OMS agent**: This is called the Microsoft monitoring agent and it is mainly used to collect logs and information from the workloads on which it is installed. It sends them back to either OMS or SCOM (if used). It's available for Windows and Linux.
- **OMS workspace**: This is the container that has stored information and configuration about the account.
- **OMS Gateway**: If you do not have an internet connection on some workloads or you have some security restrictions about exposing some workloads to an internet connection and would like them to be monitored by OMS, you can use OMS Gateway. This would then act as a proxy between your workloads and the workload itself.
- **Management solutions**: This is similar to management packs in SCOM. Mainly, it collects logs and analyzes them according to built-in rules based on best practices. It then displays them in visualizations. Moreover, it takes advantage of Azure services so you can make use of them for further actions to be done according the analyzed data. For example, if a solution is detecting that some services have stopped working, you can add an Azure automation task to start them accordingly.

Introduction to Azure Log Analytics

Monitoring has always been a cornerstone for every efficient and productive IT environment, as you will be able to get insights about what is going on in your environment and act accordingly.

Azure Log Analytics leverages the power of the cloud and gives you the best experience of running a monitoring solution on the cloud. You will not have to care about the underlying infrastructure on which the monitoring solution is running. It also provides you with a proper structure for the information it collects, where you can see visuals and meaningful insights for what you want to monitor.

Azure Log Analytics deployment models

Azure Log Analytics can be deployed in three models:

- **Directly installed agents**: You can download the OMS agent and install it and logs will be uploaded based on the solutions used in your workspace.
- **OMS Gateway**: This uses a gateway in front of your agents to act as a proxy and the gateway will be responsible for collecting the logs from the agents and sending them to Azure Log Analytics on your behalf.
- **System Center Operations Manager (SCOM) integrated**: If you integrated OMS with SCOM, you can connect the agent to SCOM and SCOM will act like OMS Gateway and send the logs to Azure Log Analytics. In this model, you will leverage features of both SCOM and OMS.

Onboarding OMS agents

In this section, you will learn how to create an OMS workspace and how to onboard agents to the Azure Log Analytics workspace

Creating the workspace

First off, you have to create the workspace on which we will onboard the agents. To do so, perform the following steps:

1. Navigate to the Azure portal and search for `Log Analytics`:

2. A new blade will be opened, where you can view the existing workspaces (if any). To create a workspace, click on **Add**:

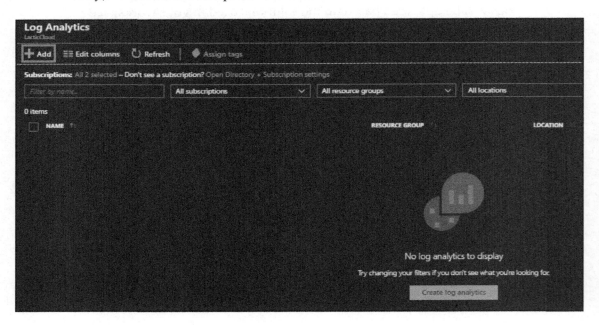

3. A new blade will be opened, where you can specify the following:

   - **Create New or Link Existing**: Select whether you want to create a new link or link to an existing one.

- **Subscription**: Select the subscription that will be charged for this service.
- **Resource group**: Select the resource group in which the workspace will exist as a resource.
- **Location**: Select the nearest location to the workloads/services you want to monitor.
- **Pricing tier**: At the time of writing, there's only one pricing tier, **Per GB,** where you will be charged according to the size of the uploaded logs. You are allowed 5 GB per month for free for data ingestion:

4. Once you are done with filling in the fields, you can click on **OK** to create the workspace.

Onboarding the agents

Once the workspace has been created, you are ready to move to the next step, where you will onboard the agents to the workspace.

To do so, perform the following steps:

1. Navigate to the workspace, where you can have an overview about it. You can also you navigate to the old portal to have a quick view of it by clicking on **OMS Portal,** which will redirect you to the portal. It will be retired by January 15, 2019:

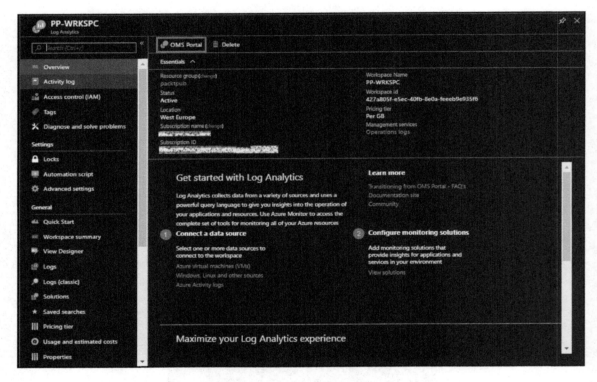

2. Under **Settings** click on **Advanced settings**, and a new blade will be opened.

3. Under **Connected Sources,** you can view the agents for **Windows Servers** and **Linux Servers**. Moreover, you can check your connections, if you have any, with **Azure Storage** and **System Center** under the same place:

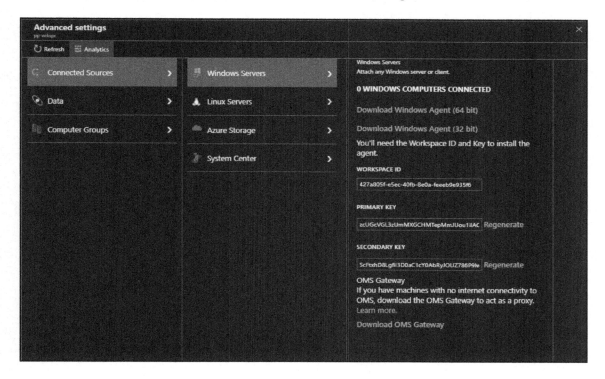

4. In this chapter, we will cover how to onboard a **Windows Server**. So, you can download the agent according to the architecture of your Windows platform, whether it is 32-bit or 64-bit, by clicking on it.

5. You can see under it **WORKSPACE ID** and **PRIMARY KEY**. Copy them, as you will need them during the installation.

6. Once the agent is downloaded, double-click on it and a new wizard will pop up, as shown in the following screenshot:

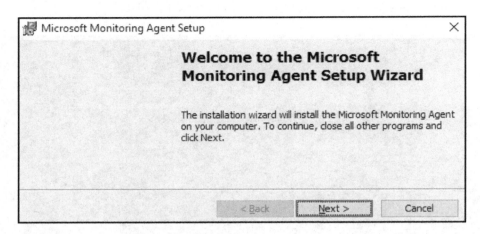

7. Click on **Next** to proceed to the next screen, where you need to read the license terms and accept them:

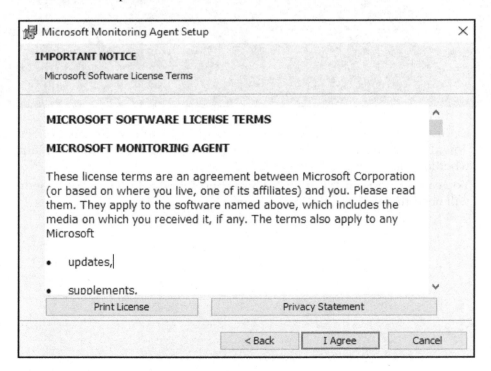

8. Once you have agreed to the license terms, you can proceed to the next screen, where you need to select the **Destination Folder** in which the agent will be installed:

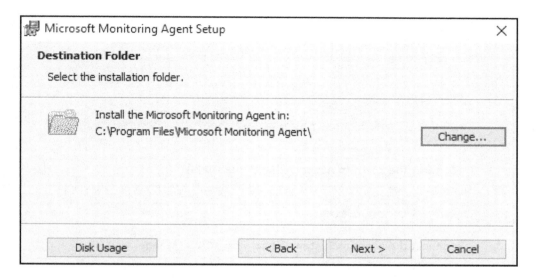

9. After that, you will have to specify which source you want to connect to (OMS or SCOM). Select according to the deployment model you will follow:

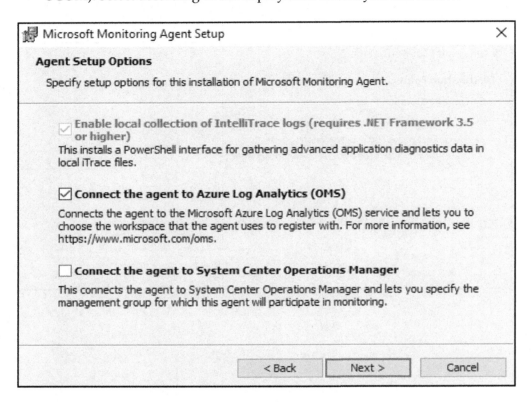

10. Then, you will have to specify the **Workspace ID** and **Workspace Key** you have copied earlier and the type of **Azure Cloud**. Leave it as **Azure Commercial** unless you are using the Azure US Government cloud, in this case, you can change it from commercial:

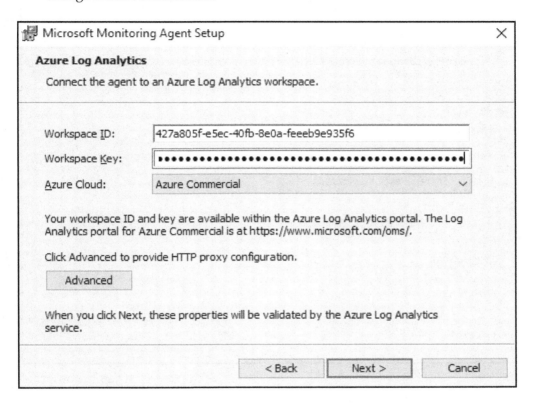

11. If you have proxies in your environment and you want to use OMS Gateway, you can click on **Advanced** and specify the **Proxy URL** and the **User Name** and **Password** if it requires authentication:

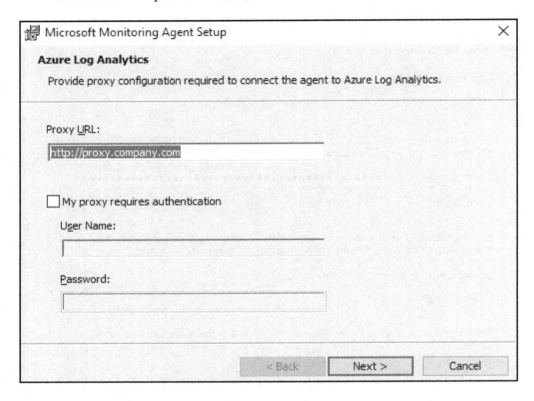

12. In the next screen, you can specify whether you want to use Microsoft Update or not:

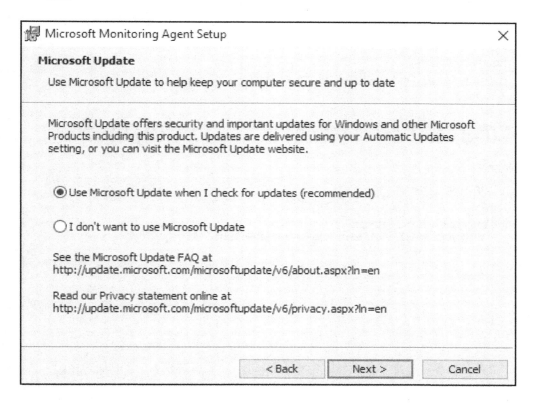

13. Finally, you will have a summary and whenever you are ready to install, click on **Install**:

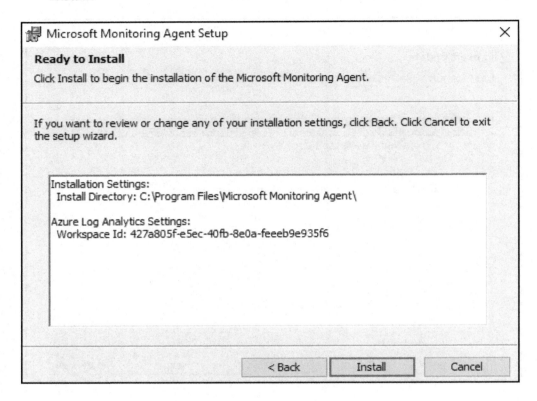

14. It will take around a couple of minutes until it is installed:

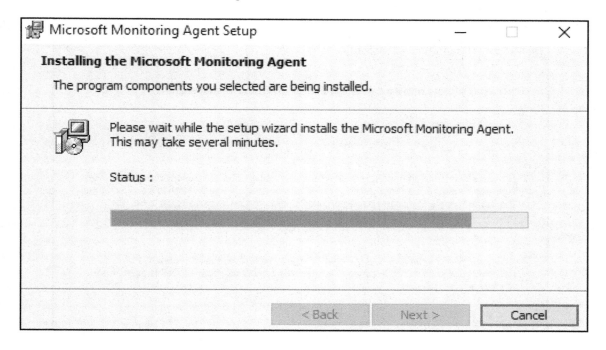

15. If it is installed successfully, this will be indicated on the wizard once it is done with the installation:

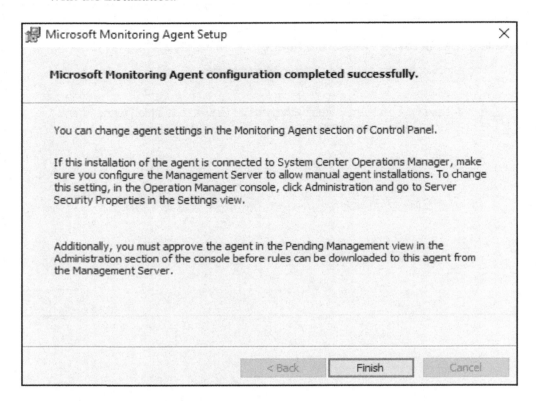

16. You can do the same process for each workload you would like to monitor. If you have bigger number of workloads, you can use System Center Configuration Manager or any other deployment tool to deploy it on them.

The agent can be installed on Windows Server 2008, at the earliest, with the latest service packs and updates installed.

Adding solutions to the workspace

Once you have the agents installed, the next step is to add solutions to monitor these workloads. To do so, perform the following steps:

1. Navigate to **Log Analytics** | **Open the workspace** | **Workspace summary**.
2. You can view any added solutions to this workspace (if any). To add a new one, click on **Add**:

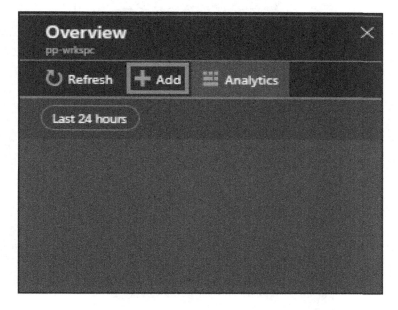

3. A new blade will be opened, where you can view solutions provided by Microsoft and partners.

4. You can scroll down and up to check the solutions and select what would fulfill your needs:

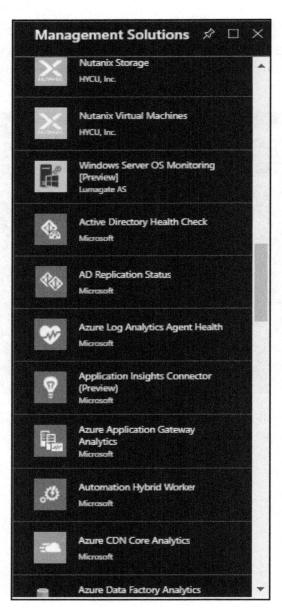

5. Once you click on the solution, a new blade will be opened, where you can select **Create**:

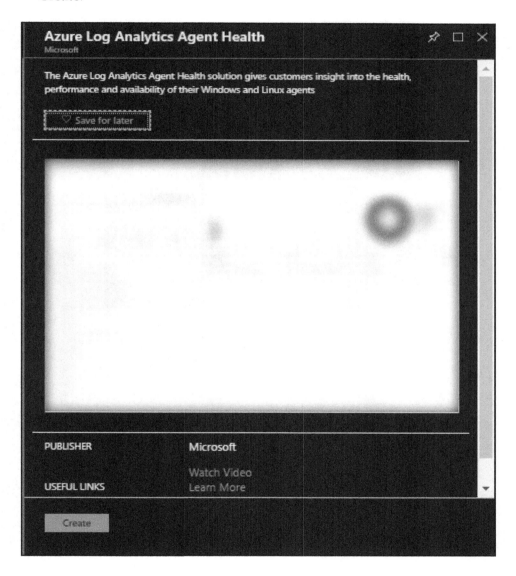

6. Then, a new blade will be opened, where you can confirm which workspace and workspace settings will be added:

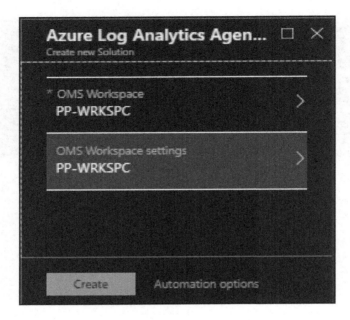

7. You can do the same for every solution you wish to add.

8. Once you are done with adding solutions, you will be able to view them in the workspace with their assessments, as shown in the following screenshot:

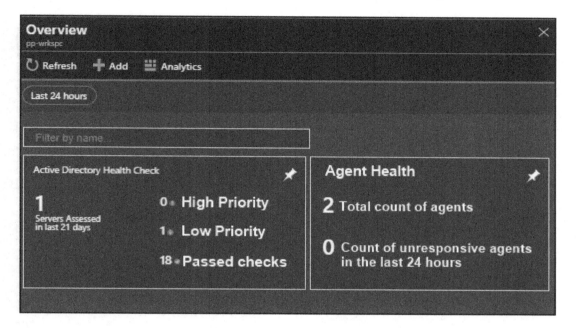

9. To get more insights about the assessments, you can click on the solution. This will open another blade displaying more details about its assessment and the recommendations you should add:

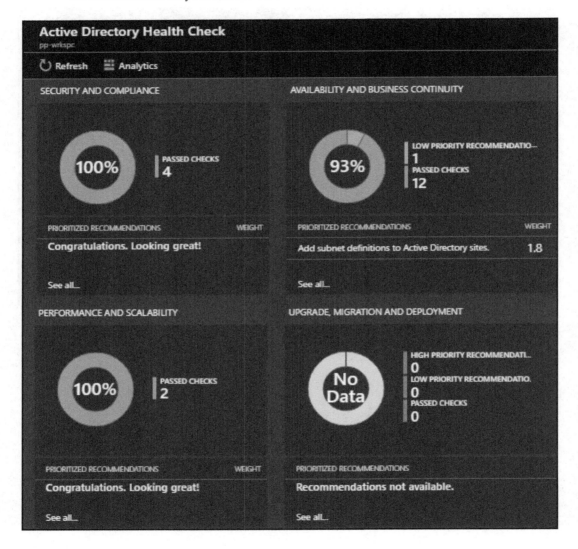

For more information about the solutions, you can check the following link: https://docs.microsoft.com/en-us/azure/azure-monitor/insights/ad-assessment.

Azure Automation

Re-implementing tasks from time to time can be tedious and time wasting. With Azure Automation, you can overcome this issue by automating all the manual, repetitive, and long-running processes.

Azure Automation is a part of OMS solutions. It gives you the ability to automate tasks across Azure Cloud, on-premises, and even other cloud platforms.

Benefits of Azure Automation

Azure Automation has many benefits. Here are some of them:

- **Time saving**: You will save a lot of time when using automation by moving away from routine and error-prone manual tasks.
- **Low costs**: The service usage itself does not cost too much. You can save many operational costs by automating your manual tasks and even automating the cleanup for your environment.
- **Heterogeneous**: Azure automation supports both Windows and Linux. Also, it is not only used with Azure Services, but also can be used with other cloud platforms and on-premises environments.

Azure Automation runbook types

A runbook looks like a container that stores your automation configuration. It is available in different types:

- **Graphical**: This type is GUI-based, where you can drag and drop tasks in a graphical editor, providing that these tasks are based on PowerShell
- **Graphical PowerShell Workflow**: This is the same as the previous type, except it is based on PowerShell Workflow

- **PowerShell**: This type is based on a Windows PowerShell scripts, where you write them in a text editor
- **PowerShell Workflow**: This is the same as the previous type, except it is based on PowerShell Workflow

- **Python**: This is the same as the previous two types, except you can write in Python instead of PowerShell

Creating an automation account

In order to get started with Azure Automation, you need to create an automation account. To do so, perform the following steps:

1. Navigate to **Azure portal** | **All Services** | and search for `Automation Accounts`:

2. A new blade will be opened, where you can view automation accounts (if any) or add new automation accounts by clicking on **Add**:

3. A new blade will be opened, where you can specify the following:

- **Name**: The name of automation account; it should be unique
- **Subscription**: The subscription that will be charged for using this service
- **Resource group**: The resource group in which it will exist as a resource
- **Location**: The region to which you want to deploy this service

- **Create Azure Run As account**: The **Azure Run As account** are mainly used to provide authentication and authorization for resources management on Azure using Azure cmdlets:

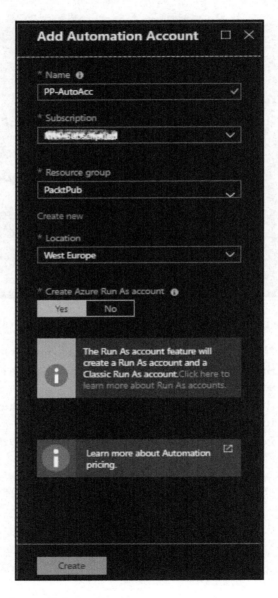

4. Once you are done, click on **Create**.

Azure runbooks

As mentioned earlier, a runbook is like the container for your automation configuration. In this section, we will check the Azure runbooks:

1. Navigate to the created automation account then click on **Runbooks** as shown in the following screenshot:

2. You can see that some sample runbooks are already there. There's also a gallery for runbooks that has many runbooks that automate some of the common tasks. To view them, click on **Browse Gallery**.

3. A new blade will be opened, where you can view the available Azure runbooks in the gallery

4. Select the runbook that you would like to add to your runbooks by clicking on it.

5. A new blade will be opened displaying the content stored within the runbook. To add it to your runbooks, click on **Import**.

6. A new blade will be opened, within which you can modify the name and description of the runbook if you wish. Then click **OK**:

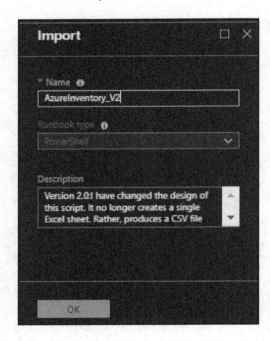

7. Navigate back to the runbooks blade and you can see it has been added:

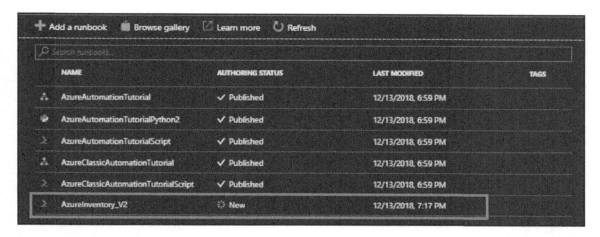

8. To deploy this runbook, click on it and a new blade will be opened displaying some basic information about the runbook:

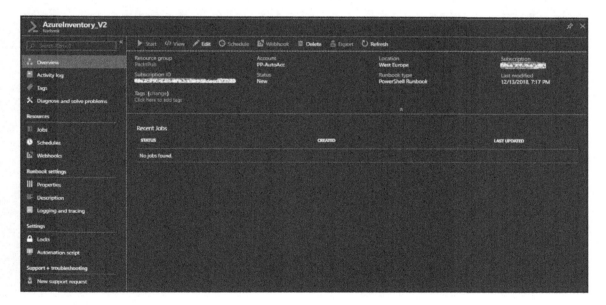

9. Then, click on **Edit** and a new blade will be opened displaying the content of the runbook:

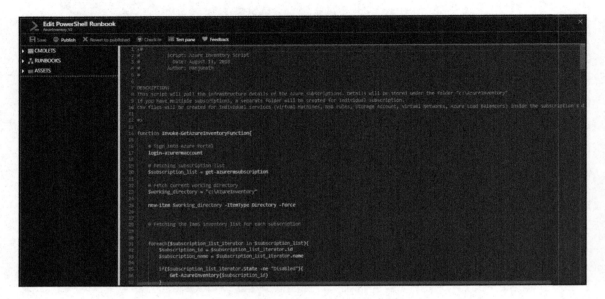

10. Within this pane, you can view the script and edit it if you wish, but do not forget to click on **Save** if you made any changes.

11. To test this script before using it regularly, you can click on **Test pane**. This will will open a new blade, where you can run this script by clicking on **Start**:

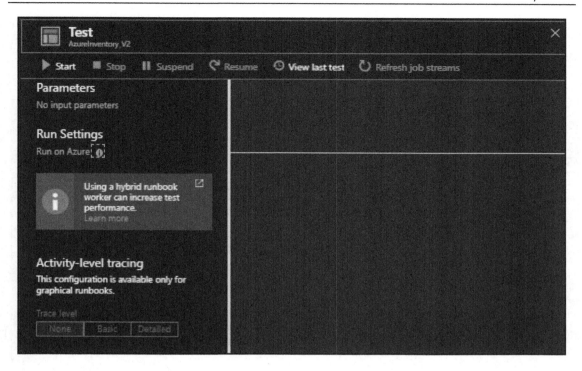

12. Once you have tested the script and have seen the expected result, you can click on **Publish,** so you can run it from runbooks normally.

Azure Automation hybrid integration

To be able to run these runbooks on workloads that are either located in on-premises or in other clouds, you need to install Hybrid Runbook Worker.

Before you proceed, ensure that OMS Agent is installed on the workload you want to install Hybrid Runbook Worker on, and the Automation Hybrid Worker solution is added to OMS Workspace. Also, navigate to the automation account and click on **Keys** to retrieve the primary key and URL, as you will need them to onboard Hybrid Runbook Worker:

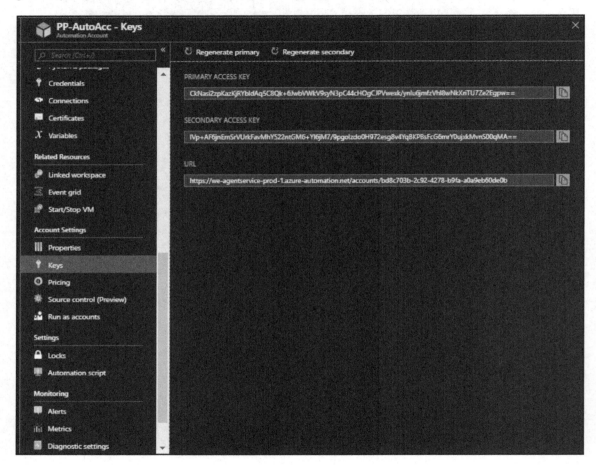

Then perform the following steps:

1. Navigate to the server you want to install the hybrid worker on and open PowerShell.
2. Navigate to the Azure Automation folder using the following PowerShell cmdlet: `cd "C:\Program Files\Microsoft Monitoring Agent\Agent\AzureAutomation\7.3.396.0\HybridRegistration"`.

3. Import the Hybrid Registration Module by running the following cmdlet: `Import-Module .\Hybri dRegistration.psd1`.

4. Then, run the following cmdlet to add it to Azure Hybrid worker groups: `Add-HybridRunbookWorker -Url <Specify the automation account URL> -Key <Specify the automation account primary key> -GroupName <Specify a name for the Hybrid worker group within which this hybrid runbook worker will run>`.

5. Then, you can navigate back to your automation account and click on **Hybrid worker groups**, and you will see that a new group has been created with a worker in it:

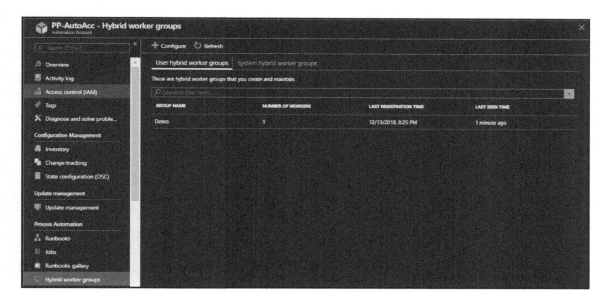

Summary

So far, you have been introduced to OMS and two of its major components (Log Analytics and Automation). This chapter was meant to give you a brief introduction and start your journey of working with OMS.

In the next and final chapter, I'll continue covering some of OMS components (Azure Recovery Services), which are designed for business continuity and disaster recovery.

Questions

1. Which of the following is not one of the major OMS solutions?
   - Azure backup
   - Log Analytics
   - Azure Application Gateway
   - Azure Site Recovery

2. You can monitor SCOM agents on OMS:
   - True
   - False

3. To be able to view the Azure Automation folder in the installation path of OMS agent, you need to:
   - Add the Automation Hybrid Worker solution to OMS Workspace
   - Create an automation account
   - Add runbooks from the gallery

Further reading

- *Integrate Operations Management Suite (OMS) with SCOM* (https://4sysops.com/archives/integrate-operations-management-suite-oms-with-scom/)
- *Integrate OMS with SCCM* (https://4sysops.com/archives/integrate-oms-with-sccm/)
- *Azure Monitor overview*: https://docs.microsoft.com/en-us/azure/azure-monitor/overview
- *Analyze Log Analytics data in Azure Monitor* (https://docs.microsoft.com/en-us/azure/azure-monitor/log-query/log-query-overview)
- *Creating or importing a runbook in Azure Automation* (https://docs.microsoft.com/en-us/azure/automation/automation-creating-importing-runbook)

11
Data Protection and Business Continuity Using OMS

Our journey is coming to an end, and I hope that it has been a beneficial one for you. In this chapter, Azure Recovery Services will be covered. First off, you will be introduced to Azure Backup and **Azure Site Recovery (ASR)**. Then, you will learn how to implement Azure Backup for Azure VMs. Finally, you will learn how to implement Azure Site Recovery to replicate on-premises Hyper-V VMs to Azure.

The following topics will be covered in this chapter:

- Introducing Azure Recovery Services
- Implementing Azure Backup
- Implementing Azure Site Recovery

Introducing Azure Recovery Services

As mentioned in the previous chapter, Azure Recovery Services is a part of the Operations Management Suite. These services provide data protection using Azure Backup and business continuity Azure Site Recovery.

Introducing to Azure Backup

Backup has always been the X factor that saves an environment from being completely damaged or lost.

Backup is one of the oldest terminologies to be heard, and it has gone through many evolutions. Nowadays, there are many vendors offering backup solutions.

In 2014, Microsoft announced that it will support backup as a service on its cloud (Azure), as a part of Azure Recovery Services, and since then, Azure Backup has undergone many enhancements.

Simply put, backing up your data to the cloud is currently one of the safest methods because of the ransomware attacks that have affected many organizations around the world.

Azure Backup can protect data at different levels, either from the cloud or from your data center, using different tools, as follows:

- **Azure Backup (Microsoft Azure Recovery Services (MARS)) agent**: This agent is responsible for backing up files and folders on Windows-based VMs. Also, it exists by default as an extension of Azure VMs, which are available in the marketplace. However, that does not deny the fact that you can install it on VMs uploaded to Azure.
- **Azure Backup Server**: This is a **System Center Data Protection Manager (SCDPM)** on Azure, and it works with all SCDPM functionalities, except disk-to-tape backup. However, Azure Backup Server integration with System Center Products is not supported at the moment. It is used to back up application workloads, such as Hyper-V VMs, VMware VMs, SharePoint Server, Exchange Server, SQL Server, and even **Bare Metal Recovery (BMR)**.
- **Azure IaaS VM Backup**: Azure VMs Backup is designed for VM-level backup, as it backs up the whole VM using a backup extension.
- **System Center DPM**: This can do the same tasks as Azure Backup Server beside the integration with other System Center Family Products.

Why Azure Backup?

Azure Backup delivers many key benefits to many environments that use it as a backup solution. Here are some of them:

- **Highly available and scalable solution**: When using Azure Backup, you do not have to worry about the underlying infrastructure on which the backup will be stored, or the maintenance of that infrastructure. Also, whenever you need to back up and keep your data on Azure, you do not have to worry about the size of the backed-up data, because no matter what the size is, Azure will handle it.
- **Self-service**: Azure Backup will allocate your backed-up data automatically without the need to assign it to a specific storage device.

- **High level of application consistency**: Azure Backup supports backing up Hyper-V, VMware VMs, SQL Servers, file servers, and so on. Whenever you restore any of these applications, you will not have to do any troubleshooting or fixing of the restored data. Therefore, you can have your application up and running shortly after restoration.
- **Multiple storage replication types**: As covered in `Chapter 2`, *Understanding Azure Storage*, storage has many replication types, which are also supported for the devices on which the backed up data will be stored:
    - **Locally redundant storage (LRS)**: This option will replicate the backed-up data three times to other storage devices within the same data center
    - **Geo-redundant storage (GRS)**: This option will replicate the backed-up data to another data center in another region

- **Higher level of security**: For a higher level of security, Azure provides data encryption for the transmission of data to and from the cloud using an encryption passphrase. The encryption passphrase is stored locally, not on the cloud, and whenever you need to restore the data, you can use that passphrase.
- **Retain your data forever:** Traditionally, long-term backups were kept on tapes, but on Azure, you can keep your data as long as you wish.

Introducing to Azure Site Recovery

Business continuity is one of the most important key points, especially for enterprises. Building a disaster recovery site is a must-do step to take to have an optimal environment. That is why Microsoft Azure provides ASR services, which can be used to build your disaster recovery site.

This service helps to ensure that your applications are up and running all the time, even if a disaster happens to your data center.

When using ASR, you can build your own disaster recovery site for your Azure VMs, your on-premises VMs and/or physical servers, or even manage replication between a primary and secondary site.

In March 2015, Microsoft announced the launch of ASR and, since then, this service has undergone many enhancements and added features according to customer feedback.

ASR supportability

At the time of writing, ASR supports replication from the following sources:

- Hyper-V Server 2012 R2 and 2016
- vSphere/vCenter 5.5, 6.0, 6.5, and 6.7
- Physical servers

Hyper-V servers

As mentioned earlier, you can only replicate Hyper-V VMs from Windows Server 2012 R2 and Windows Server 2016. However, if you are managing your Hyper-V hosts with **System Center Virtual Machine Manager (SCVMM)**, you can use it to replicate VMs from Hyper-V hosts.

At the time of writing, SCVMM 2012 R2 and 2016 are the supported versions to work with ASR.

> You need to install the latest updates for your Hyper-V hosts and SCVMM to avoid any issues during replication. Also, you need to make sure that your SCVMM 2016 cloud does not support the co-existence of Windows Server 2016 and Windows Server 2012 R2 hosts. If there are any configurations that include the upgrade from SCVMM 2012 R2 to 2016, it will not be supported.

The following table specifies the supported and unsupported configurations for Hyper-V hosts and guests during replication:

	Supported	Unsupported
Guest OSes	You can check the following link to see the supported OSes: `https://docs.microsoft.com/en-us/azure/cloud-services/cloud-services-guestos-update-matrix`	Any OS that is not mentioned on the previous link is not supported
Hyper-V network configurations	• NIC teaming • VLANS • IPv4	IPv6
Guest network configurations	• IPv4 • Static IP address for Windows-based VMs • Multiple NICs for the same VM • IPv6 (if SCVMM is not used)	• IPv6 (If SCVMM is used) • NIC teaming • Static IP addresses for Linux-based VMs
Azure network configuration for Hyper-V guests	• Express route • Internal and external load balancers • Traffic manager • Multiple NICs • IPv4 • Reserved IPs • You can retain your source IP addresses • Azure Virtual Network service endpoints (without Azure Storage firewalls)	Accelerated networking
Hyper-V host storage configurations	• SMB 3.0 • SAN (iSCSI) • Multipath I/O (MPIO)	None

Hyper-V guest storage configurations	• VHD and VHDX • Generation 2 VMs • EFI and UEFI • Total storage for the VM not more than 4,095 providing that no VHD should exceed 1 TB • Disk: 4K logical and 512 bytes physical sector • **Logical Volume Management (LVM)**. LVM is supported on data disks only. Azure provides only a single OS disk • You can have a volume with a striped disk with a size of more than 1 TB. • LVM logical volume management is supported for Linux-based VMs • Storage spaces • Disk exclusion • MPIO	• SMB 3.0 • Shared cluster disk • Encrypted disk • Disk: 4K logical and physical sector
Azure Storage configurations for Hyper-V guests	• LRS, GRS, and RA-GRS • Premium storage • Encryption at rest (**Storage Service Encryption (SSE)**)	• Cool and hot storage • Azure import/export service • Block Blobs • Azure Storage firewalls for virtual networks configured on target storage/cache storage account (used to store replication data)
Azure compute configurations for Hyper-V guests	• Availability sets service • **Hybrid User Benefit (HUB)** • Managed disks service (for failover)	Managed disks service is not supported when failing back to on-premises

VMware vSphere and physical servers

As mentioned earlier, you can use Azure as a DR site for your VMware vSphere and physical servers. However, you have to ensure that the versions of VMware vSphere are 5.5, 6.0, 6.5, or 6.7 and the same goes for vCenter if you want to replicate from it:

	Supported	Unsupported
VMware guest machines and physical server OSes	The following Windows-based OSes: • Windows Server 2008 R2 SP1 • Windows Server 2012 • Windows Server 2012 R2 • Windows Server 2016 The following Linux-based OSes: • Red Hat: 5.2 to 5.11, 6.1 to 6.10, 7.0 to 7.5 • CentOS: 5.2 to 5.11, 6.1 to 6.10, 7.0 to 7.5 • Debian 7, 8 • SUSE Linux Enterprise Server 11 SP3, SP4 • SUSE Linux Enterprise Server 12 SP1,SP2,SP3 • Ubuntu 14.04, 16.04 LTS server • Oracle Enterprise Linux 6.4, 6.5, 6.6, 6.7, 6.8, 6.9, 6.10, 7.0, 7.1, 7.2, 7.3, 7.4, 7.5 which run either a Red Hat compatible kernel or Unbreakable Enterprise Kernel Release 3	Other OSes are not supported
VMware hosts/physical server network configurations	• NIC teaming is supported for VMware • VLANs • IPv4	• IPv6 • NIC teaming is not supported for physical servers
VMware guests/physical servers network configurations	• IPv4 • Static IP addresses (on the failback they will be set to DHCP) • Using multiple NICs for the same VM	• IPv6 • NIC teaming
Azure network configurations for VMware guests/physical servers	• Express route • Internal and external load balancers • Traffic manager • Multiple NICs • IPv4 • Reserved IPs • You can retain your source IP addresses • Azure Virtual Network service endpoints (without Azure Storage firewalls)	Accelerated networking

VMware hosts/physical servers storage configurations	• NFS is supported for VMware hosts • SAN (iSCSI/FC) • vSAN (VMware) • MPIO • Host Virtual Volumes (VVols)	NFS (physical server)
VMware guests/physical servers storage configurations	• VMDK • Disk Exclusion • EFI/UEFI (at least Windows Server 2012) • RDM (VMware) • Total storage for the VM/Server not more than 4,095 providing that no disk should exceed 1 TB • Disk with 4K logical and 4K physical sector size • Disk with 4K logical and 512 bytes physical sector size • You can have a volume with a striped disk with a size of more than 1 TB. • LVM logical volume management is supported for Linux-based VMs	• Shared cluster disk • Encrypted Disk • NFS • SMB 3.0 • Storage spaces • Hot add and remove for disks • MPIO
Azure Storage configurations for VMware guests/physical servers	• LRS, GRS, and RA-GRS • Premium storage • Encryption at rest (SSE)	• Cool and hot storage • Block Bbobs • Azure Import/Export service • General purpose v2 storage accounts • Azure Storage firewalls for virtual networks configured on target storage/cache storage account (used to store replication data)
Azure compute configurations for VMware guests/physical servers	• Availability sets service • HUB • Managed disks service	None

The following are the Linux-based OSes:

- Debian 7, 8 for the following kernel versions: `https://docs.microsoft.com/en-us/azure/site-recovery/vmware-physical-azure-support-matrix#debian-kernel-versions`
- Linux Enterprise Server 12 SP1,SP2,SP3 for the following kernel versions: `https://docs.microsoft.com/en-us/azure/site-recovery/vmware-physical-azure-support-matrix#suse-linux-enterprise-server-12-supported-kernel-versions`
- Ubuntu 14.04, 16.04 LTS server for the following kernel versions: `https://docs.microsoft.com/en-us/azure/site-recovery/vmware-physical-azure-support-matrix#ubuntu-kernel-versions`

Although UEFI is supported for VMware VMs to be failovered to Azure, at the time of writing, failback to on-premises is not supported. Moreover, no more than four partitions on the OS disk of this VM should exist, and at least Mobility Service version 9.13 should be installed.

Implementing Azure Backup

In this section, we will go through a step-by-step guide to implement one of the Azure Backup solutions (Azure IaaS VM Backup).

Creating an Azure Recovery Services vault

Before backing up your data, you have to do some configuration, such as building a Recovery Services vault, which is the place where the backed-up data will be stored. Once you have done that, you can start backing the data up. To do so, perform the following steps:

1. Navigate to **All Services** and search for **Recovery Services Vault:**

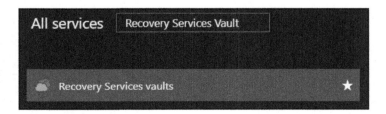

2. A new blade will be opened where you can view the current recovery service vaults (if any). Click on **Add** to create a new one:

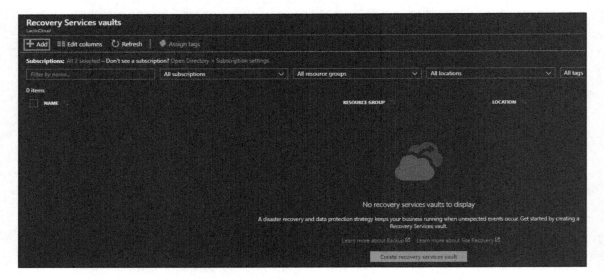

3. A new blade will be opened where you can specify the following:
   - **Name**: A descriptive name for the vault.
   - **Subscription**: The subscription that will be charged for using this service.

- **Resource group**: The resource group in which the vault will exist as a resource.
- **Location**: Select the nearest location for your services:

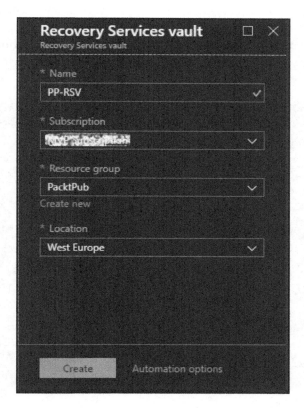

4. Once you are done, click on **Create**.

Backing up an Azure VM

With the Recovery Services vault created, you are ready to start backing up the VM:

1. Navigate to the Recovery Services vault that you have just created, and click on **Backup**

2. To start the backup process, you can click on the **Backup** button on the console, or navigate to **Backup** under **GETTING STARTED** in the navigation pane, as shown in the following screenshot:

3. Once you have clicked on **Backup**, a new blade will pop up, asking about the following:

   - **Where is your workload running?** You have only two options: **Azure** or **On-premises**

   - **What do you want to backup?** This depends on the answer to the previous question

     - If your workload is running on Azure, you will have **Virtual machine**, **Azure FileShare (Preview)**, and **SQL Server in Azure VM (Preview)** as choices, as shown in the following screenshot:

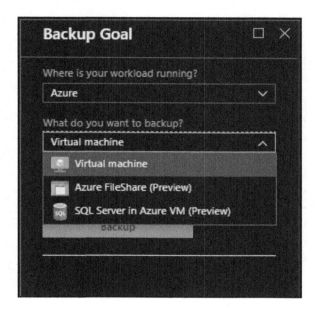

- If your workload is running **On-Premises**, you can choose one or more of the following: **Files and folders**, **Hyper-V Virtual Machines**, **VMware Virtual Machines**, **Microsoft SQL Server**, **Microsoft SharePoint**, **Microsoft Exchange**, **System State**, and **Bare Metal Recovery**, as shown in the following screenshot:

4. Since our workload is a **Virtual machine** running on Azure, I think you know which options we will select, and once they have been selected, we will click on **Backup**, as shown in the following screenshot:

5. Once you have clicked on **Backup**, a new blade will pop up where you can specify your backup policy, which includes **BACKUP FREQUENCY** and **RETENTION RANGE**, as shown in the following screenshot:

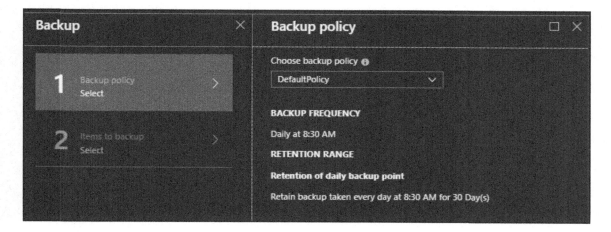

6. The policy shown in the previous screenshot is a default policy that takes a backup daily at 08:30. and retains it for 30 days. Yet, you can create your own customized policy by selecting **Create New**:

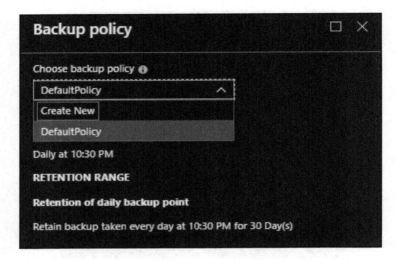

7. Once you have clicked on **Create New**, you will have to specify the **Policy name**, **Backup frequency**, and **Retention range** according to your needs, as shown in the following screenshot:

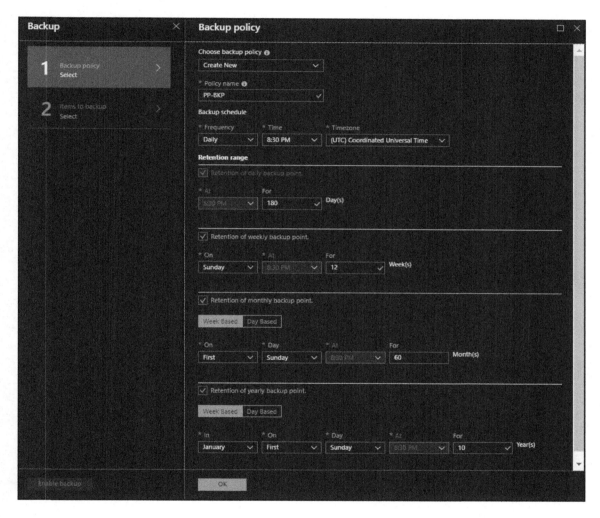

8. Once you are done with your configurations, click **OK**.

9. Once you have clicked on **OK**, you will be navigated to a new blade in which you have to specify the virtual machines you need to back up, as shown in the following screenshot:

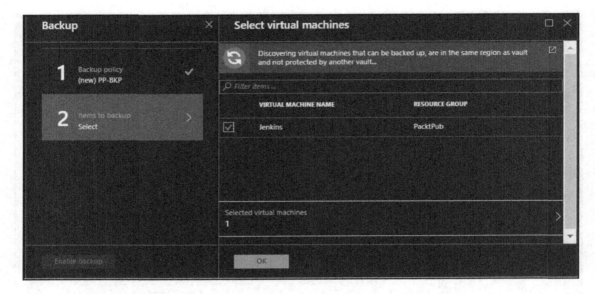

10. Then, click on **OK** and **Enable Backup** and your backup will be triggered.

Implementing Azure Site Recovery

In this section, we will go through how to implement Azure Site Recovery for Hyper-V hosts to replicate to Azure Site Recovery. However, before you get started, make sure you have virtual networks and storage accounts created on Azure so they can be used when the VMs/physical servers are failovered to Azure.

Like Azure Backup, a Recovery Services vault will be needed. In this scenario, we will use the same Recovery Services vault.

Preparing the infrastructure for replication

In this section, we will go through the required steps to prepare your infrastructure for replication:

1. Navigate to **Azure portal** | **All Services** | **Recovery Services vault** | and select the Recovery Services vault that will be used for ASR.

2. To get started with the replication process, you have to navigate to **Site Recovery** under **GETTING STARTED** in the navigation pane, as shown in the following screenshot:

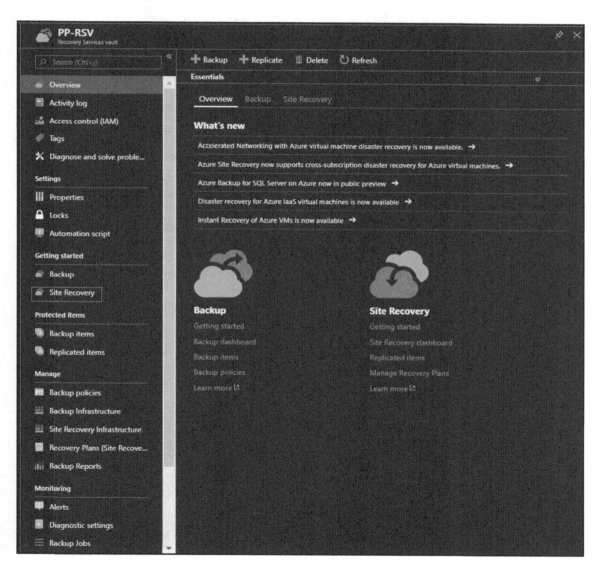

3. A new blade will be opened displaying the steps to go through. So, you have to click on **Prepare Infrastructure**:

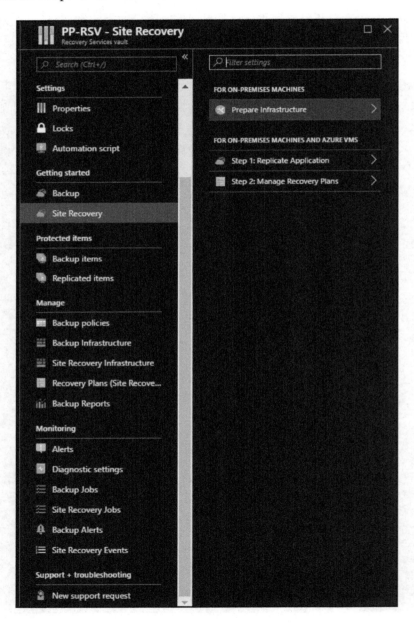

4. A new blade will be opened with the steps you have to do to prepare your infrastructure. The first step is to specify the protection goal, which will ask you to specify the following:

- **Where are your machines located?**: You can selected either **On-premises** or **Azure**. If Azure is selected, you will not have to proceed any further in the preparation, because you can start replication from Azure VMs to ASR with no infrastructure preparation, as it is already on Azure.

- **Where do you want to replicate your machines to?**: You can replicate to Azure or another recovery site and in this case ASR will act as a replication orchestrator between the recovery sites.

- **Are your machines virtualized?**: Select **Yes, with Hyper-V**, as this is what we are going to implement for this scenario.

- **Are you using System Center VMM to manage your Hyper-V hosts?**: Specify whether you are using SCVMM to manage it:

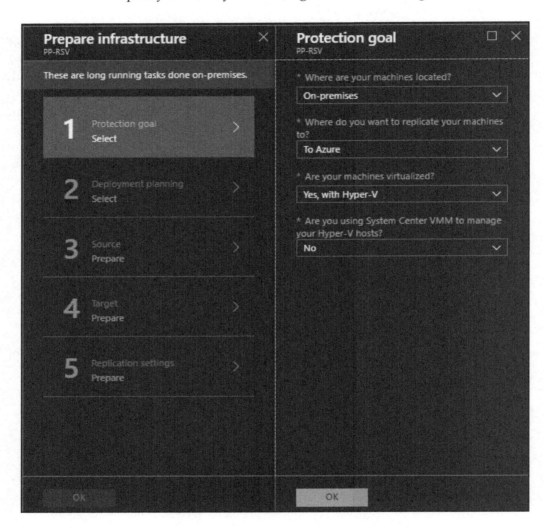

5. The next step is to confirm that you have done a deployment planning. To do so, you can download the tool mentioned in the following screenshot and run it on your hosts:

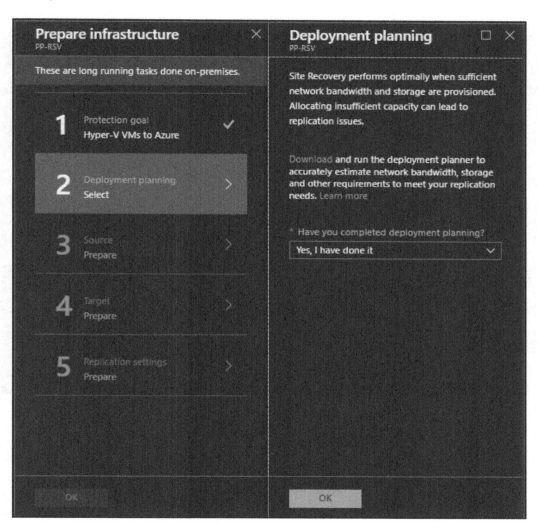

6. After that, you need to prepare the source. To do so, you need to specify a Hyper-V site, which will act as a logical container for your Hyper-V hosts. If you do not have any, click on **Hyper-V Site** and create a new one, as shown in the following screenshot:

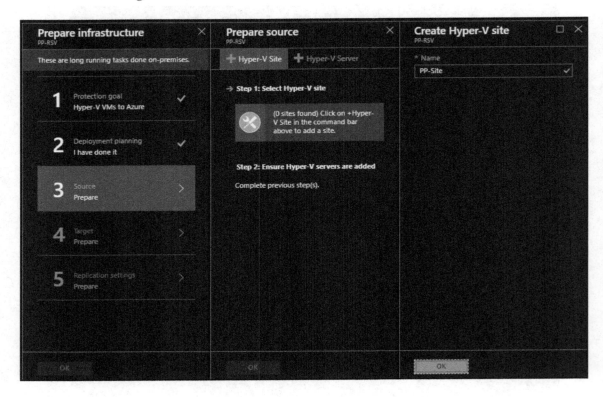

7. Then, you need to put onboard your **Hyper-V Hosts**. To do so, you need to download the installer for Microsoft Azure Site Recovery Provider, and the vault registration key, as shown in the following screenshot:

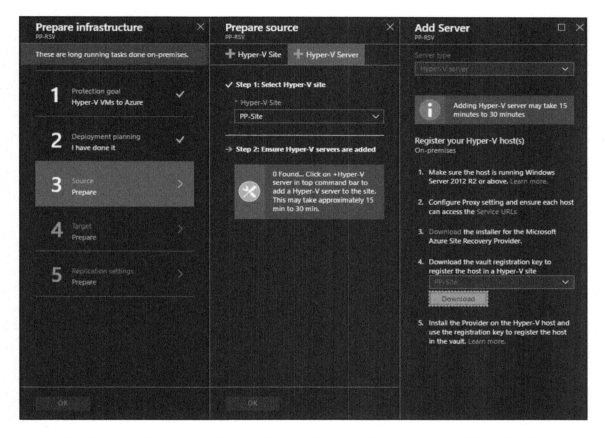

8. Once you have downloaded the installer and the registration file on the Hyper-V hosts, run the installer.

9. A new wizard will be opened where you can specify whether you want to turn on updates for Microsoft Windows and other software:

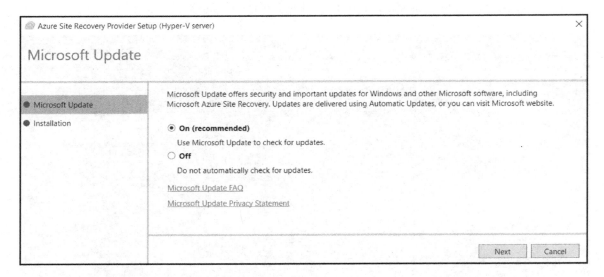

10. In the next screen, you can specify the install path for the provider:

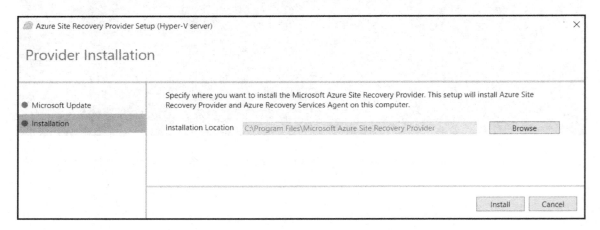

11. Once the installation is done, you can start to register it by clicking on **Register**:

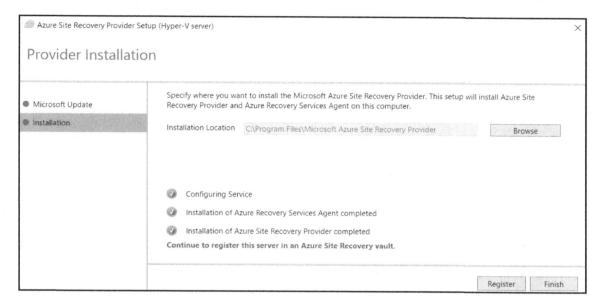

12. A new wizard will be opened where you can browse for the registration key file, and it will automatically retrieve the subscription, vault name, and Hyper-V site name:

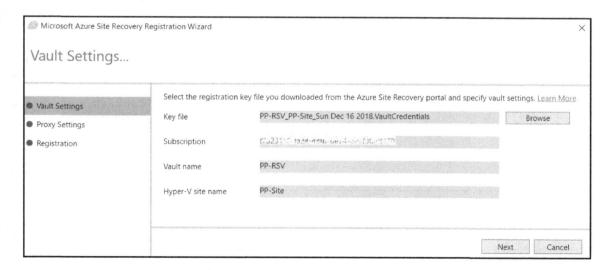

13. In the next step, you can specify whether you have a proxy. If so, you need to configure it properly:

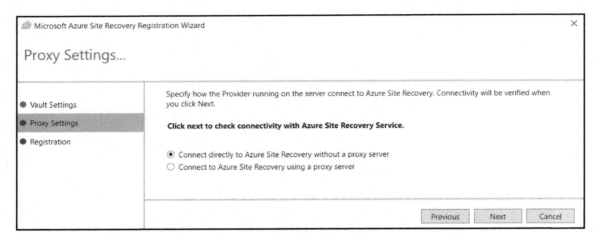

14. When you click on **Next,** it will start registering the Hyper-V host in the Azure Recovery Services vault:

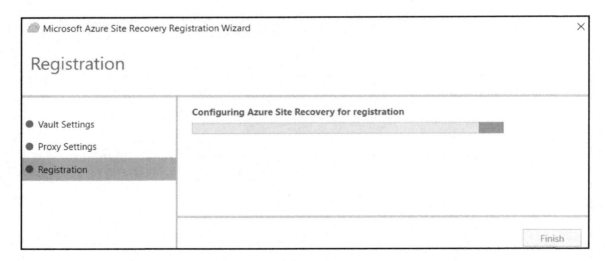

15. Finally, it will display if the registration has been successful:

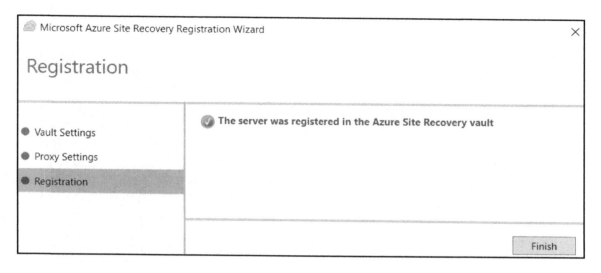

16. Now, you can get back to the Azure portal to the last blade you were working on. If it did not detect the Hyper-V host, you can refresh the page or start the process on the portal again, and it will be detected:

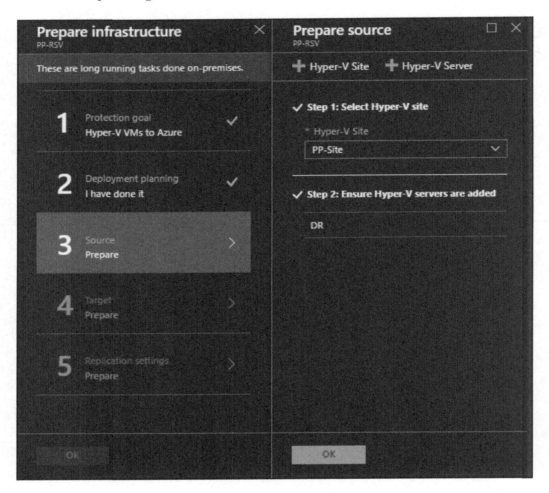

17. You will be navigated to the next blade to specify the target by specifying the following:

- **Subscription**: The subscription that will be charged for usage when the machines failover to ASR.
- **The deployment model used after failover**: It's recommended to the resource manager model for your IaaS for your resources to operate in when they failover to Azure.

- **Storage account**: The storage account within which your VMs storage will be stored. If you do not have any, you can click on **Storage account** to create one.
- **Networks**: The VNet that will be used for your machines after failover. If you do not have any, you can click on **Network** to create one:

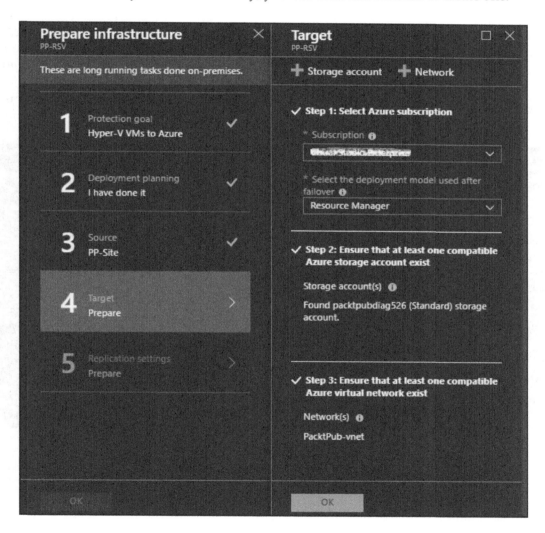

18. Finally, you need to specify the replication policy. If you do not have any, you can click on **Create and Associate**, and a new blade will be opened, where you need to specify the following:

- **Name**: The name of the policy
- **Copy frequency**: Specify how frequently data should be synchronized between source and target locations
- **Recovery point retention in hours**: Number of hours up to which the recovery points will be retained
- **App-consistent snapshot frequency in hours**: Frequency at which an application consistent snapshot is taken for the VMs
- **Initial replication start time**: The time at which the initial replication will be kicked off:

19. Once you have finished, click on **OK**.

Enabling the replication

With the infrastructure prepared, you are ready to trigger the replication. To do so, perform the following steps:

1. Navigate to **Step 1: Replication Application**.
2. You will be prompted to configure the source and the source location, **Hyper-V Site**:

3. Then, you will need to specify the settings for the machines that will run on Azure after the failover, as shown in the following screenshot:

4. Then, you can select the VMs you want to replicate:

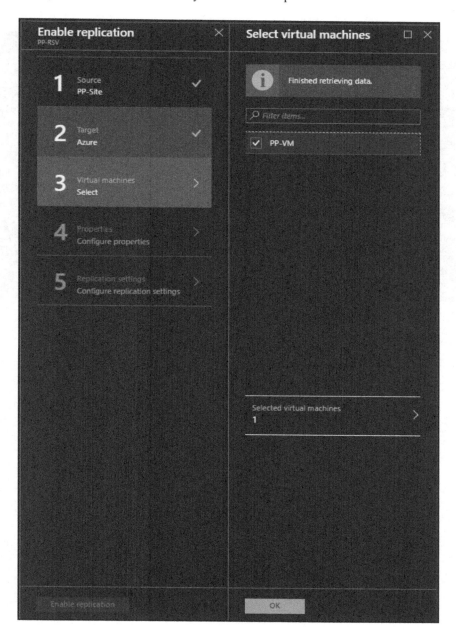

5. After that, you can specify some configuration for the VM, such as OS type, OS disk, and which disks to replicate:

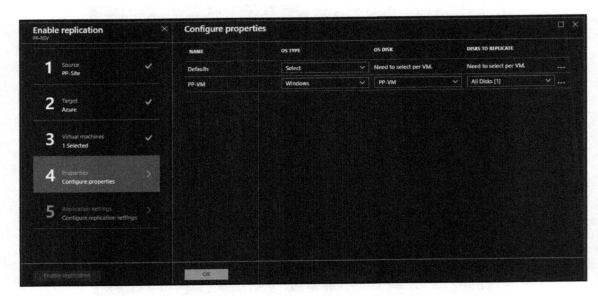

6. Finally, you can specify the replication policy:

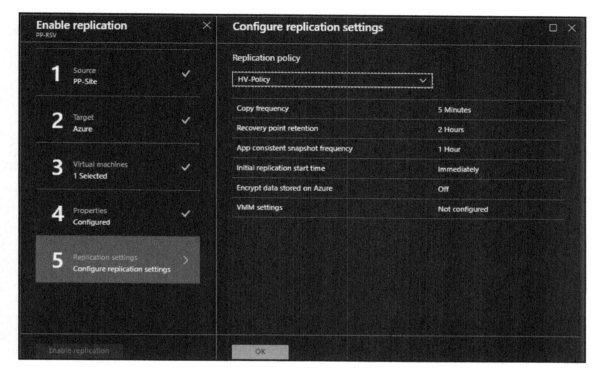

7. Once you have finished, you can click on **OK** and **Enable replication**, and the initial replication will be triggered.

Summary

This chapter continued to cover one of OMS' greatest services: Azure Recovery Services. As you have learned from this chapter, you should be able to protect your data with Azure Backup and keep your business continuity using Azure Site Recovery.

It's been a nice journey to cover some of the basics about Microsoft Azure so far, and how to work with the most common services. I hope you have gained the knowledge you wished for from this book, and I'd like to thank you for reading it.

Questions

1. Which of the following Azure backup solutions can integrate with System Center products?
    - Azure Backup Server
    - System Center Data Protection Manager
    - Both of them

2. Which of the following services can work without the Recovery Services vault?
    - Azure Site Recovery
    - Log Analytics
    - Azure Backup
    - None of them

3. Accelerated Networking is not supported for the machines replicated from on-premises to ASR:
    - True
    - False

Further reading

- *Install Azure Backup Server* (https://4sysops.com/archives/how-to-install-azure-backup-server/)
- *Azure Backup Server post-installation tasks* (https://4sysops.com/archives/azure-backup-server-post-installation-tasks/)
- *About Azure Migrate* (https://docs.microsoft.com/en-us/azure/migrate/migrate-overview)
- *Create and customize recovery plans* (https://docs.microsoft.com/en-us/azure/site-recovery/site-recovery-create-recovery-plans)
- *Set up the source environment for VMware to Azure replication* (https://docs.microsoft.com/en-us/azure/site-recovery/vmware-azure-set-up-source)
- *Azure Site Recovery Tips & Tricks - Part 2* (https://vlacticcloud.wordpress.com/category/azure/oms-azure-site-recovery/)
- *Azure Backup Tips & Tricks - Part 4* (https://vlacticcloud.wordpress.com/category/azure/oms/azure-backup/)

Assessments

Chapter 1: Microsoft Azure 101

1. True
2. False
3. False
4. False
5. True
6. True
7. Automation tools:
   - Azure PowerShell
   - Azure CLI

Chapter 2: Understanding Azure Storage

1. True
2. True
3. False
4. False
5. False
6. True

Chapter 3: Getting Familiar with Azure Virtual Networks

1. False
2. True
3. True
4. True

Chapter 4: Understanding Azure Virtual Machines

1. Stopped
2. A-Series
3. Temporary Disk
4. VMs in the same availability set should have at least two NICs

Chapter 5: Starting with Azure Web Apps Basics

1. Function apps and logic apps
2. All of them
3. False

Chapter 6: Managing Azure Web Apps

1. True
2. Connection strings
3. Scaleout
4. Storage account

Chapter 7: Basics of Azure SQL Database

1. True
2. Spanning Databases
3. The statements are:
    - If an Azure Web App is using Azure SQL Database as a backend, you will have to allow access to it by adding firewall rules for the IP addresses of the web app.
    - You can connect to Azure SQL Database from another Azure subscription without adding firewall rules.

Chapter 8: Managing Azure SQL Database

1. False
2. Active Directory – SSPR
3. The database size is not important during database recovery
4. The conditions are:
   - It is not a gateway subnet
   - There are no service endpoints enabled for it
   - The subnet is not used by any other service
   - At least 16 IP addresses are available in the subnet

Chapter 9: Understanding Azure Active Directory

1. Support for domain join for different OSes
2. 30 days
3. True

Chapter 10: Monitoring and Automating Azure Services Using OMS

1. Azure Application Gateway
2. True
3. Add Automation Hybrid Worker solution to OMS workspace

Chapter 11: Data Protection and Business Continuity Using OMS

1. System Center Data Protection Manager
2. Log Analytics
3. True

Other Books You May Enjoy

If you enjoyed this book, you may be interested in these other books by Packt:

Implementing Azure Cloud Design Patterns
Oliver Michalski, Stefano Demiliani

ISBN: 978-1-78839-336-2

- Learn to organize Azure access
- Design the core areas of the Azure Execution Model
- Work with storage and data management
- Create a health endpoint monitoring pattern
- Automate early detection of anomalies
- Identify and secure Azure features

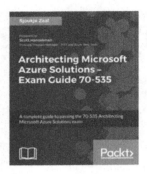

Architecting Microsoft Azure Solutions - Exam Guide 70-535
Sjoukje Zaal

ISBN: 978-1-78899-173-5

- Use Azure Virtual Machines to design effective VM deployments
- Implement architecture styles, like serverless computing and microservices
- Secure your data using different security features and design effective security strategies
- Design Azure storage solutions using various storage features
- Create identity management solutions for your applications and resources
- Architect state-of-the-art solutions using Artificial Intelligence, IoT, and Azure Media Services
- Use different automation solutions that are incorporated in the Azure platform

Leave a review - let other readers know what you think

Please share your thoughts on this book with others by leaving a review on the site that you bought it from. If you purchased the book from Amazon, please leave us an honest review on this book's Amazon page. This is vital so that other potential readers can see and use your unbiased opinion to make purchasing decisions, we can understand what our customers think about our products, and our authors can see your feedback on the title that they have worked with Packt to create. It will only take a few minutes of your time, but is valuable to other potential customers, our authors, and Packt. Thank you!

Index

A

address space
  adding, to Azure Virtual Networks 82
App Service application settings
  about 156, 157, 159
  key points 160, 161
  reference 160
App Service plan scaleup
  key points 163
App Service plan
  about 134
  creating 141, 142, 144
  dedicated infrastructure plans 135
  key points, for autoscaling 170
  scaling out, automatically 165, 167, 169
  scaling out, manually 164, 165
  standard infrastructure plans 134
App Service
  creating 145, 146, 147, 148, 150
Azure Active Directory authentication
  setting 201, 204
Azure AD, flavors
  basic 225
  free 225
  Premium P1 225
  Premium P2 226
Azure AD
  about 223, 224
  benefits 224
  flavors 225
Azure App Service Environments
  about 135
  creating 137, 138, 139, 140
  offerings 136
Azure App Services 133
Azure App Services backup

about 171, 172
  key points 173
Azure App Services scalability
  about 161
  scale up approach 161, 162
  scaleout approach 164
Azure automation tools
  about 28
  Azure CLI 30
  Azure PowerShell 29
Azure Automation
  about 275
  automation account, creating 276, 277, 278
  Azure runbooks 279, 280, 281, 282
  benefits 275
  hybrid integration 283, 285
  runbook types 275, 276
Azure Backup
  about 288
  advantages 289
  Azure Recovery Services vault, creating 295, 297
  Azure VM, backing up 298, 299, 300, 301, 302, 303, 304
  implementing 295
Azure CLI 30
Azure CLI 2.0
  installing 30, 32
Azure hybrid benefit
  reference 102
Azure IaaS VM Backup 288
Azure Log Analytics
  about 255
  deployment models 255
Azure portal experience
  about 15, 26
  Azure cloud shell 22

Azure portal settings 23
  dashboard 17
  hub 19
  notifications 21
  portal 16
  settings 25
  signing up 15
Azure PowerShell
  about 29
  installing, from PowerShell Gallery 29
  module, installing 29
Azure pricing calculator
  reference 37
Azure Recovery Services vault
  creating 295, 297
Azure Recovery Services
  about 287
  Azure Backup 288, 289
  Azure Site Recovery 290
Azure Resource Manager (ARM)
  about 27
  benefits 27
  key points 28
Azure Site Recovery (ASR)
  about 290
  Hyper-V servers 290
  implementing 304
  infrastructure, preparing for replication 304, 305,
    306, 307, 310, 311, 312, 313, 314, 315, 316,
    318
  replication, enabling 319, 322, 323
  replication, implementing 320
  supportability 290
  VMware vSphere and physical servers 293
Azure SQL Database (PaaS)
  about 177
  scenarios 177
Azure SQL Database business continuity
  about 205
  active geo-replication 211
  auto-failover groups 214, 216
  deleted database, restoring 209, 211
  hardware failure 206
  point-in-time restoration key points 209
  point-in-time restore 206, 209

  working 205
Azure SQL Database
  about 175
  accessing, server-level firewall used 188, 190
  accessing, SQL SSMS used 190
  connecting to 187
  creating 181, 182, 184, 185, 186
  Elastic database pools 178
  features 176
  single databases 179
  SQL database managed instance 179
  types 178
Azure SQL Managed Instances
  about 216
  advantages 216
  connecting to 219
  creating 217
  key points 219
  types 216
Azure storage accounts
  about 41
  Blob storage account 41
  creating 43, 45, 47
  general-purpose storage account v1 41
  general-purpose storage account v2 42
  tips 43
Azure Storage architecture
  about 68
  frontend layer 69
  partition layer 69
  sparse storage 69
  stream layer 69
  TRIM 70
Azure Storage services
  about 47
  Blob storage 47
  file storage 63
  Queue storage 59
  Table storage 54
Azure Storage types
  about 36
  performance 40
  persistency 40
Azure Storage
  about 35

benefits 36
Azure virtual machines
    about 96
    backing up 298, 299, 300, 301, 303, 304
    creating 99, 100, 101, 102, 103, 105, 106,
        107, 108, 109, 110
    data disk, adding to 115
    data disks 120
    data disks, managing 116, 117, 119
    disks, resizing 120
    host caching 121, 122
    network interface card, adding 124, 125
    series 98
    service level agreements (SLAs) 97
    statuses 96
Azure Virtual Networks services
    about 83
    NICs 89, 90
    public IP 83
    public IP address, creating 84, 85
    public IP prefix, creating 87, 88
    service endpoints 92
Azure Virtual Networks
    about 73, 74
    address space, adding 82
    benefits 74, 75
    considerations, for Azure VMs 130
    creating 75, 76, 77
    gateway, adding to 81
    subnet, adding 78, 79
Azure VM networking
    about 122
    inbound rules 123
    NICs, configuring 126, 127, 129
    outbound rules 123
Azure VM series
    reference 98
Azure VM storage
    about 111
    managed disks 111, 112
Azure Web Apps 134

B

Bare Metal Recovery (BMR) 288
Blob storage account

about 41
cool access tier 42
hot access tier 42
premium access tier 42
Blob storage
    about 47
    append blobs 48
    block blobs 48
    creating 48, 50, 51, 52, 53
    key points 53, 54
    page blobs 48

C

cloud computing
    advantages 6
    features 7
cloud deployment models
    about 8
    hybrid cloud 10
    private cloud 8
    public cloud 9
cloud services
    about 14
    Infrastructure as a service (IaaS) 14
    Platform as a Service (PaaS) 14
    Software as a Service (SaaS) 14
Common Internet File System (CIFS) 63

D

data disk
    adding, to Azure virtual machines 115, 116,
        118, 119
database 175
Database Transaction Units (DTUs)
    reference 179
dedicated infrastructure plans, App Service
    basic 135
    isolated 135
    premium 135
    standard 135
deployment models, Azure Log Analytics
    directly installed agents 255
    OMS Gateway 255
    System Center Operations Manager (SCOM)
        integrated 255

deployment slots
  about 153
  adding 154
  key points 155, 156
Distributed and Replicated File System (DFS) 69
DTU service tiers 179
durability, Azure Storage
  about 36
  replication types 37

E

elastic database pools
  about 178
  benefits 195
  creating 196
  database, adding 198
elastic Database Transaction Units (eDTUs)
  reference 179

F

file storage
  about 63
  advantages 63
  creating 64, 65, 66, 67
  key points 68
first-in, first-out (FIFO) model 59

G

gateway subnet
  adding, to Azure Virtual Networks 81
general-purpose storage account v1 41
general-purpose storage account v2 42
Geo-redundant storage (GRS)
  about 39, 289
  advantages 39
  drawbacks 39
groups, Azure AD
  creating 234, 239
  working with 234

L

Locally redundant storage (LRS)
  about 37, 289
  advantages 38

drawbacks 37
Logical Volume Management (LVM) 292

M

Microsoft Azure
  china regions 12
  cloud computing, evolution 6
  cloud deployment models 8
  cloud platform 8
  Germany regions 12
  government regions 12
  overview 6
  public regions 10
  regions 10
  subscriptions 13
Microsoft SLAs, Azure VMs
  reference 97
Multi-Factor authentication 246, 248

N

network interface card (NIC)
  adding, to Azure VM 124

O

OMS agents
  about 255
  onboarding 258, 259, 260, 261, 262, 263, 264,
    266, 267, 268
  solutions, adding to workspace 269, 270, 271,
    272, 273, 274
  workspace, creating 256, 257
OMS
  about 253
  agent 254
  features 253, 254
  Gateway 254
  management solutions 254
  terminologies 254
  workspace 254
Operations Management Suite (OMS) 253

P

PartitionKey 55
performance, Azure Storage

premium storage 40
standard storage 40
persistency, Azure Storage
non-persistent storage 41
persistent storage 40
Platform as a Service (PaaS) 175
private cloud
advantages 9
disadvantages 9
public cloud
advantages 9
disadvantages 10

Q

Queue storage
about 59
creating 60, 61, 62
key points 62

R

Read-access geo-redundant storage (RA-GRS)
about 39
advantages 39
drawback 39
replication types, Azure
Geo-redundant storage (GRS) 39
Locally redundant storage (LRS) 37
Read-access geo-redundant storage (RA-GRS)
39
Zone redundant storage (ZRS) 38
Reserved Instances, Azure VMs
reference 96
role-based access control (RBAC) 27
RowKey 55
runbook types, Azure Automation 275

S

series, Azure VM
A-Series 98
B-Series 98
D-Series 98
E-Series 98
F-Series 98
G-Series 98
H-Series 98

L-Series 98
M-Series 98
N-Series 98
Server Message Block (SMB) 63
server-level firewall
used, for accessing Azure SQL Database 188,
190
service tier types
about 179
DTU service tiers 179
shared infrastructure plans, App Service
free 134
shared 134
Single sign-on (SSO) 224
Software as a service (SaaS) 133, 195
SQL Database (IaaS/PaaS) 177
SQL on Azure VMs (IaaS)
about 178
scenarios 178
SQL SSMS
used, for accessing Azure SQL Database 190
subnets
adding, to Azure Virtual Networks 78, 79
System Center Data Protection Manager (SCDPM)
288
System Center Virtual Machine Manager
(SCVMM) 290

T

Table storage
about 54
creating 56, 57, 58
key points 58
PartitionKey 55
RowKey 55
timestamp 55
tasks, Azure AD
about 240
custom domain name, configuring 248, 250
Multi-Factor Authentication 246, 248
self-service password reset 240, 243
users sign-in activities 244

U

users, Azure AD
 creating 226, 228, 231
 deleted users 233
 password, resetting 232
 working with 226

V

vCore service tiers
 business critical 181
 general purpose 180
 hyperscale 180
virtual machines 19
virtual memory systems (VMS) 5
virtualization 6

VM disks
 data disk 113
 OS disk 113
 temporary disk 113

W

workspace, OMS agents
 creating 256
 solutions, adding 269, 271, 274

Z

Zone redundant storage (ZRS)
 about 38
 advantages 38
 drawbacks 38

Made in the USA
Columbia, SC
29 August 2020